MIGRANTS
FOR EXPORT

MIGRANTS FOR EXPORT

How the Philippine State Brokers Labor to the World

Robyn Magalit Rodriguez

 University of Minnesota Press
Minneapolis
London

The University of Minnesota Press gratefully acknowledges the financial assistance provided for the publication of this book from the University Research Council at The State University of New Jersey, Rutgers.

Portions of chapter 5 were previously published as "Domestic Debates: Constructions of Gendered Migration from the Philippines," in *Borders on Belonging: Gender and Immigration*, ed. Neferti Tadiar, special issue, *Scholar and Feminist On-Line* (2008); http://www.barnard.edu/sfonline/immigration/.

Published by the University of Minnesota Press
111 Third Avenue South, Suite 290
Minneapolis, MN 55401-2520
http://www.upress.umn.edu

Library of Congress Cataloging-in-Publication Data

Rodriguez, Robyn Magalit.
    Migrants for export : how the Philippine state brokers labor to the world /
Robyn Magalit Rodriguez.
        p.   cm.
    Includes bibliographical references and index.
    ISBN 978-0-8166-6527-3 (hc : alk. paper) –
    ISBN 978-0-8166-6528-0 (pb : alk. paper)
        1. Foreign workers, Philippine. 2. Migrant labor. 3. Manpower policy – Philippines.
    4. Philippines – Emigration and immigration.   I. Title.
    HD6305.F55R63 2010
    331.6'2599 – dc22   2009053623

Printed in the United States of America on acid-free paper

The University of Minnesota is an equal-opportunity educator and employer.

18   17   16   15   14   13   12   11   10   9   8   7   6   5   4   3   2

Contents

Abbreviations

APEC	Asia Pacific Economic Cooperation
ASEAN	Association of South East Asian States
BAYAN	Bagong Alyansang Makabayan
BES	Bureau of Employment Services
BLA	Bilateral Labor Agreement
CFO	Commission on Filipinos Overseas
CNMI	Commonwealth of the Northern Mariana Islands
DFA	Department of Foreign Affairs
DH	domestic helper
DOLE	Department of Labor and Employment
EO	Executive Order
EOI	Export Oriented Industrialization
EPZ	Export Processing Zone
EVP	Exchange Visitor Program
GABRIELA	General Assembly Binding Women for Reforms, Integrity, Equality, Leadership, and Action
GFMD	Global Forum on Migration and Development
GPB	Government Placement Branch
HRD	Human Resources Development
HSPA	Hawaiian Sugar Planters' Association
ILAS	International Labor Affairs Service
ILO	International Labor Organization
IMA	International Migrants Alliance
IMF	International Monetary Fund
INFO	International Network of Filipinos Overseas
IOM	International Organization for Migration
ISO	International Organization for Standardization
IT	Information Technology
JCM	Joint Commission meetings
KMU	Kilusang Mayo Uno (May First Movement)

LINKAPIL	Lingkod Sa Kapwa Pilipino (Link for Philippine Development program of the Commission on Filipinos Overseas [CFO])
LMI	Labor Market Information
MI	Migrante International
MOH	Ministry of Health
MOU	Memorandum of Understanding
MTPDP	Medium Term Philippine Development Program
NBI	National Bureau of Investigation
NGO	nongovernmental organization
NIC	newly industrializing country
NLRC	Nationalism Labor Relations Commission
NSB	National Seaman's Board
NSO	National Statistics Office
OCW	Overseas Contract Worker
OEDB	Overseas Employment Development Board
OFI	Overseas Filipino Investor
OFW	Overseas Filipino Worker
OPA	Overseas Performing Artist
OWWA	Overseas Workers Welfare Administration
P.D. 442	Presidential Decree 442
PDOS	Pre-Departure Orientation Seminar
PDSP	Pre-Departure Showcase Preview
POEA	Philippine Overseas Employment Administration
POLO	Philippine Overseas Labor Office
RA 8042	Republic Act 8042
SABIC	Saudi Basic Industries
SAP	Structural Adjustment Program
SHPT	Special Hiring Program for Taiwan
SME	Small and Medium-Sized Enterprises
SOFA	Status of Forces Agreement
SWS	Social Weather Stations
TESDA	Technical Education and Skills Development Authority
UN	United Nations
VFA	Visiting Forces Agreement
WB	World Bank
WTO	World Trade Organization

Introduction

Neoliberalism and the Philippine Labor Brokerage State

*Not only am I the head of state responsible for a nation of 80 million people.
I'm also the CEO of a global Philippine enterprise of 8 million Filipinos who
live and work abroad and generate billions of dollars a year in revenue for
our country.* — President Gloria Macapagal-Arroyo, May 2003

A "Global Enterprise" of Labor

During a state visit to the United States in 2003, Philippine President
Gloria Macapagal-Arroyo aggressively encouraged U.S. businesspeople to hire Philippine workers to fill their employment needs in
the territorial United States and beyond. When American coloniz-
ers encountered Filipinos in 1898, they considered them a backward
and savage lot who were, nevertheless, sufficiently educable. The
United States proceeded to violently conquer the Filipino people
and then, with a policy of "benevolent assimilation," schooled them
into being proper colonial subjects who could labor for the nascent
empire. Arroyo assures her audience that American colonial education
adequately served its purpose and even exceeded it.[1]

Today, Arroyo suggests, the Filipino is a thoroughly modern and
civilized global worker who can labor anywhere and under any set of
circumstances for American as well as other employers. The president insists that Philippine workers can be relied upon to labor for
the contemporary U.S. empire, pledging that Philippine workers will
"play a role in helping rebuild the land for the people of Iraq." No

matter how difficult or dangerous a place of employment may be, Filipinos and Filipinas are ever-willing workers. Employers can even be spared the expense of training workers because it is a task done in the Philippines, one that the Philippine government has "worked hard to support." Though not stated explicitly by the president, her speech does suggest that employers can save on labor costs because Philippine workers are a temporary workforce ostensibly less able or willing to demand wage increases or better benefits over time. In short, the promise of the Philippine worker is not merely the promise of a worker of good quality, but ultimately one who is cheap.

According to Arroyo, she is not merely president but also the "CEO" of a profitable "global enterprise" that generates revenues by successfully assembling together and exporting a much sought-after commodity worldwide: "highly skilled, well-educated, English-speaking" as well as "productive" and "efficient" workers. By calling herself a "CEO" Arroyo represents herself not as a head of state but as an entrepreneur, the ideal neoliberal subject, who rationally maximizes her country's competitive advantage in the global market. I suggest that the Philippines, especially when it comes to migrants, is a labor brokerage state.

Labor brokerage is a neoliberal strategy that is comprised of institutional and discursive practices through which the Philippine state mobilizes its citizens and sends them abroad to work for employers throughout the world while generating a "profit" from the remittances that migrants send back to their families and loved ones remaining in the Philippines. The Philippine state negotiates with labor-receiving states to formalize outflows of migrant workers and thereby enables employers around the globe to avail themselves of temporary workers who can be summoned to work for finite periods of time and then returned to their homeland at the conclusion of their employment contracts. As Antonio Tujan of IBON (a nonprofit research-education-information development institution), a longtime critic of the government's labor export program, puts it, the Philippine state engages in nothing more than "legal human trafficking."[2]

Figure 1. *Brochure produced by the Philippine Overseas Employment Administration.*

If, as many scholars have argued, global capital demands "flexible" labor, Philippine migrants are uniquely "flexible" as short-term, contractual, and incredibly mobile workers. Employers of Philippine workers need not "race to the bottom" by relocating to the Philippines but can actually stay in place as Philippine workers can be conveyed directly to them. The Philippines offers a reserve army of labor to be deployed for capital across the planet.

The Philippine state, in fact, distinguishes itself in its capacity to facilitate the out-migration of its population to destinations spanning the planet. It is undeniably the world's premier "global enterprise" of labor as the Philippine migrant worker has become practically ubiquitous around the globe. The worldwide distribution of Philippine migrants is staggering and perhaps unmatched by any other labor-sending country.[3] According to the most recent (2008) statistics from the Philippine Overseas Employment Administration (POEA) one of the key institutions in the Philippine government's transnational migration apparatus, 1,236,013 Filipino and Filipina workers were deployed in some 200 countries and territories around the globe. These workers joined the millions of Philippine migrants already employed overseas to total an estimated 8,233,172.[4] With a population of over 80 million people, that means that nearly 10 percent of the Philippine population is working abroad.

Among newly deployed migrants, the top occupations in which Philippine migrants are employed are the following (in order): household service workers; waiters, cleaners, and related workers; charworkers, cleaners, and related workers; nurses, professional; caregivers and caretakers; laborers/helpers, general; plumbers and pipe fitters; electrical wiremen; welders and flame-cutters; building caretakers.[5] Both men and women leave the country although in the past decade women's out-migration has outpaced the out-migration of men. However, statistics collected from April to September 2008 indicate that 51.6 percent of migrants were men while 48.4 percent were women. One in four migrants were between the ages of twenty-five and twenty-nine, and one-third were unskilled.[6]

Philippine migrants' global mobility occurs in the face of increasing immigration restrictiveness around the world. Many countries are strengthening their borders, especially against those hoping to immigrate and settle with their families.[7] In spite of this trend, out-migration from the Philippines continues to increase. The Philippine state has been central to the globalization of Filipina and Filipino workers. While people from the Philippines actively seek out opportunities to live and work overseas for a variety of reasons, ultimately the countries they imagine as possible sites for temporary sojourns as well as the jobs they apply for are determined in large part by the Philippine state's labor brokerage strategy.[8]

President Arroyo, for example, played a vital role in securing new jobs for Philippine workers in the Middle East to support U.S. military operations. After meeting U.S. businessmen, she met U.S. government officials to discuss the two countries' shared interests in the global "war on terror" and, it can be assumed, transfers of Philippine labor, for not long after her brief stint in the United States, Iraq was added to the ever-growing list of Philippine migrants' countries of destination. Moreover, according to a report by the POEA published shortly after President Arroyo's U.S. visit, ten thousand to fifteen thousand jobs were expected to open even beyond Iraq in countries including Kuwait, Bahrain, and Qatar because of expected "billion dollar infrastructure development projects in the Middle East (gas, electricity, water, finance, communications, engineering design, retail, health services, construction, IT, hotel/tourism)," attributed "to the presence of US forces."[9]

If the Philippine state facilitates the out-migration of its citizens, just as importantly it attempts to shape its overseas citizens' economic and political connections to the Philippines. The Philippines' "profitability" as a "global enterprise" hinges on its ability to maintain its overseas citizens' relations to the homeland. Labor brokerage requires a particular set of relations between state and citizen. Under a migration regime of labor brokerage, Philippine citizens are to leave their families behind in the Philippines while giving themselves over to employers in faraway destinations. At the same time, they are to continue being linked to the homeland, especially through their remittances, as the foreign exchange generated by migrants' overseas wages has become vital to the Philippine economy. In 2008

Product	Earnings
Electronic products	$1.915 billion
Remittances	$1.494 billion
Articles of apparel and clothing accessories	$125 million
Coconut oil	$80 million

Figure 2. Earnings from the three top export products compared with remittances for the month of July 2009. Sources: POEA, National Statistics Office (NSO).

alone, migrants remitted over U.S.$16 billion through official banking channels.[10] It is true that the very structure of the migrant labor system functions in such a way that individuals working overseas necessarily remit their earnings to their dependents left behind in the Philippines.[11] Still, the state invests heavily in channeling migrants' remittances back to the Philippines, with special emphasis on securing their remittances through official banking channels as well as state-sponsored development projects.

The Philippine state's transnational migration apparatus has become something of an "export-processing zone" that assembles and mobilizes and exports a commodity, workers, that actually rivals other export commodities in terms of profitability. A comparison of earnings from the Philippines' top three highest earning export products with remittances in the month of July 2009 indicates that remittances from migrants are second only to electronic products (Figure 2). In other words, in the Philippines the export of people can be more profitable than the export of clothing.

It is because Philippine migrants are short-term employees that labor-receiving countries source their workers from the Philippines. The Philippine state's future deployments of migrants (and ultimately remittances), therefore, depend on its ensuring that migrants are compliant with the terms of their employment contracts. In other words, the Philippine government requires that migrants return home to the Philippines immediately upon the completion of their work. The Philippine state's investments in its relations to its citizen-workers globally are crucial for accomplishing that task.

This book examines how and why the Philippine state has emerged as a "global enterprise" of labor. It uses a case study of the Philippines to understand contemporary processes of neoliberal globalization. As Neferti Tadiar argues, "The Philippines is, as a supplier of global labour, a constitutive part of the world-system."[12] A key objective here is to map what Saskia Sassen calls a "countergeography of globalization," that is, a form of globalization "either not represented or seen as connected to globalization," yet is "deeply imbricated in some of the major dynamics constitutive of globalization."[13]

My findings draw on qualitative methods including ethnographic research of the government's migration bureaucracy, interviews with state officials and migrants, and archival work of government documents conducted over the course of the last decade.[14] I examine the mechanisms by which the Philippine state mobilizes, exports, and regulates migrant labor to meet worldwide gendered and racialized labor demand. At the same time, I examine how the state has reconfigured Philippine citizenship and produced novel invocations of Philippine nationalism to normalize its citizens' out-migration while simultaneously fostering their ties to the Philippines. Though I begin with a quote from the Philippine president, this book is fundamentally about the quotidian institutional and discursive practices of the state.[15]

To get at why the Philippines has become a global broker of labor and the kind of functions it performs in the contemporary global order, however, requires first an understanding of how neoliberal globalization has reshaped the role of states more broadly and an understanding of the new forms of labor demand engendered by contemporary globalization. I turn to a discussion of the existing scholarship on the state and globalization and international migration in the sections that immediately follow.

Brokering Labor as a Neoliberal Strategy

Neoliberalism, "Development," and the Nation-State

Under conditions of neoliberal globalization, the forms and functions of the nation-state have been shifting quite dramatically. While many scholars have lamented the eclipse of the state by the forces of global capital, many others suggest that what we are apprehending is in fact its reconfiguration. Rather than being hollowed out, the state has created new apparatuses by which to actually facilitate neoliberalism. As David Harvey argues, the neoliberal state seeks out "internal reorganizations and new institutional arrangements that improve its competitive position as an entity vis-à-vis other states in the global market."[16] In her critique of Harvey Aihwa Ong suggests, first, that neoliberalism, although hegemonic globally, should not be understood as having common, universalized consequences. She further argues that "rather than taking neoliberalism as a tidal wave of market-driven phenomena that sweeps from dominant countries to smaller ones, we could more fruitfully break neoliberalism down into various technologies."[17]

Neoliberal orthodoxy consequently takes different shapes in different states. Moreover, it requires that states develop an arsenal of strategies to meet its imperatives. In the Philippines, for instance, the state has introduced numerous measures to create "new institutional arrangements" necessary to neoliberal globalization. Like other developing countries, it has complied with the mandates of what critics of neoliberalism have called the "Washington Consensus," which involves privatization, deregulation, and liberalization among other sets of economic reforms or "structural adjustments."[18] But unlike other states in the global South, the Philippines has crafted a strategy of labor brokerage by which it mobilizes and deploys labor for export to profit from migrants' remittances. Remittances from migrants' overseas employment has strengthened the government's foreign exchange reserves, helping the Philippines pay off the onerous debts it has incurred from lenders like the World Bank and the International Monetary Fund, along with a host of private banks, as a consequence of structural adjustment programs.

The Philippine state is not, however, simply a passive actor in the global order as elites at its helm have enthusiastically implemented policies compliant with the neoliberal Washington Consensus. Developing countries "are undertaking restructuring and serve the needs of transnational capital not simply because they are 'powerless' in the face of globalization, but because a particular historical constellation of social forces now exists that present an organic social base for this global restructuring of capitalism."[19]

Neoliberalism in the Philippines and other formerly colonized areas needs to be understood within the context of legacies of imperialism. For the Philippines neoliberal strategies of the state have long been shaped by its status as a neocolony of the United States. One can argue that neoliberalism in the formerly colonized global South is a contemporary form of coloniality.[20]

In a neocolonial, neoliberal state like the Philippines, labor brokerage functions to address the failures of so-called "development."[21] It is a peculiar kind of "trickle up" development as individual migrants' earnings abroad become a source of foreign capital for the Philippine state. The Philippine state remains committed to drawing direct investments from foreign capital through neoliberal economic reforms; however, it also heavily draws on "investments" from its very own citizens. The strategy of labor brokerage merely "perpetuates the conditions this policy claims to ameliorate and reinforces the IMF structural adjustment policies' grip on Philippine underdevelopment since remittances mainly go to debt servicing rather than to generating new local employment projects," as Ligaya McGovern suggests.[22] It is still a cornerstone of Philippine neoliberal "development" today. As E. San Juan acerbically, though accurately, puts it, the globalization of Philippine workers "is primarily due to economic coercion and disenfranchisement under the retrogressive regime of comprador-bureaucratic (not welfare-state) capitalism."[23]

Neoliberal Governmentality

Though neoliberalism is characterized by a set of economic rationalities, as distilled in the Washington Consensus, neoliberalism is also a technology of governmentality. Aihwa Ong, drawing from Foucauldian understandings, suggests that neoliberalism is a mode of governing populations. She argues that the "neoliberal politics of 'shrinking' the state are accompanied by a proliferation of techniques to remake the social and citizen-subjects."[24] By brokering labor, the Philippine state attempts to contain the multiple social dislocations that are the consequence of its aggressive implementation of neoliberal economic policies. It represents employment abroad and remittances as the fulfillment of a new form of nationalism. Contemporary Philippine citizenship has become a modality of governmentality.

The consequences of the neoliberal Washington Consensus have been disastrous for ordinary people in the Philippines, as they have been for most people throughout the world as they face increasingly precarious conditions of employment (if they are employed at all) and the elimination of state services.[25] In the Philippines, structural adjustment has resulted in currency devaluation (meant to be an enticement for foreign investors), which has reduced real incomes in the Philippines, making it difficult for people to cope with the rising costs of living, which include the burden of having to pay for what were once state-subsidized public services. As the already small middle class tries to maintain its tenuous status, the difficulty of everyday life for the working classes and the poor compel many to join up with militant leftist movements, both legal and underground, to contest the state's neoliberal orientation.[26] Economic and political elites in the Philippines are all too familiar with the sorts of explosive upheavals these tensions can give rise to.

When the state's neoliberal policies are coupled with charges of graft and corruption, as was the case for President Joseph Estrada in 2001, mass protests can bring an administration down. Overseas jobs address Philippine citizens' dire need for livable wages and arguably contain social unrest to some extent.[27] Under conditions of globalization, elites have to deal with "the contradictory pressures of (global) accumulation and (national) legitimation. This enduring contradiction is being managed by a restructuring of the capitalist state and a realignment of internal power relations within national state apparatuses."[28] Successive Philippine presidents have offered up the promise of employment (albeit overseas) during the bleakest economic crises to calm citizens' growing anxieties about job prospects, and in the Philippines labor brokerage is an important legitimization scheme for the state.

Of course, states' legitimacy is not confined to the national arena. According to Aihwa Ong, developing and newly industrializing states concern themselves with accumulating status and recognition in the global context.[29] Social prestige in the world order is also gendered as well as racialized. L. H. M. Ling argues that "biological males (the 'native man'), masculinized conventions ('Third World state'), and even socioeconomic systems ('developing economies') can be feminized if they are viewed as backward, weak, or poor — traits conventionally associated with femininity" and, it can be argued, with nonwhiteness.[30] "The accumulation of capital, the organization of the labor process, the construction of the modern nation-state," as Winant argues, was "all fashioned in the global racial workshop."[31] Represented by neighboring Asian leaders and economists as Asia's perennial failure,[32] the Philippine state is invested in recuperating its feminized status through policy interventions that conform to hegemonic white, masculinized global conventions.

It is within the context of tremendous uncertainty that the government's relentless pursuit of neoliberal restructuring has produced the Philippine state's promotion of overseas employment among its citizens. Employment abroad allows Philippine citizens to earn incomes far greater than would be possible in the Philippines (in part because the peso is so devalued) and therefore sustain their families' well-being, at least for the immediate future. There is something quintessentially neoliberal about labor brokerage as a technology of government. It requires the responsibilization of Philippine citizens who are to directly bear the costs of neoliberal restructuring as their remittances go to debt servicing. Moreover, as the Philippine state withdraws social supports and thereby passes on the costs of education, health care, and other expenses to its citizens, brokering labor absolves the state from having to provide services directly to its citizens. Ordinary people are forced to bear sole responsibility for the costs associated with newly privatized services with the wages they earn abroad.

The labor brokerage state simultaneously extends new kinds of "rights" and benefits to its overseas citizens. New iterations of citizenship, what might be termed oxymoronically enough *migrant citizenship,* become a means by which the state deftly masks how the entitlements of Philippine citizenship are in fact dwindling under conditions of neoliberalism. Since its inception, the Philippine state's migration regime has included provisions that are supposed to protect migrants from exploitative working conditions as well as entitlements reserved only for overseas workers. These protections promise, for example, the Philippine state's extraterritorial intervention in contractual disputes workers may have with their employers. As women's migration began to outpace men's migration and moral panics about the absence of mothers from their families proliferated, the state also created mandatory training programs for women seeking employment in what have been officially categorized by the government as "vulnerable" occupations (domestic work and "entertainment").[33] Migrants are eligible for skills training and upgrading while they are abroad and when they return to the Philippines. Their children can even qualify for scholarship funds. In fact, overseas employment itself is cast as a "right" of Philippine citizens, which the state pledges to guarantee.

Migrant citizenship is aimed at placating migrants' fears about being vulnerable as foreign workers abroad. It is a reactive measure to Philippine citizens' transnational protests against the unjust treatment of migrants at the hands of foreign employers and governments through migrant citizenship. The state pledges particular kinds of protections and entitlements to secure legitimacy for its migration program among it citizens — both those who leave as well as those who stay. By offering migrants what is essentially a portable set of "rights," the state can represent itself as a caring and virtuous state committed to its citizens. Moreover, through migrant citizenship, the Philippine state can secure the legitimacy of labor brokerage as a strategy on an international scale as rights regimes are a hallmark of democratic governance, necessary for acceptance into the fraternity of nation-states. For the most part, migrant citizenship comes with few guarantees, yet it becomes an important technique by which the Philippine state reshapes its relations to its citizens under conditions of neoliberal globalization.

If the Philippine state has reconfigured citizenship, it has necessarily rearticulated ideas of nationalism and national belonging for the purposes of brokering labor. After all, in a society where people are forced to secure their livelihoods far from their families and country of birth, ideas of "home" and "the nation" are destabilized. With the increasing importance of overseas employment, the Philippine state has come to represent migrants as "new national heroes." Rather than denigrating out-migration as a "brain drain" (and therefore some kind of nationalist betrayal) or employing punitive methods to force migrants to remit their earnings back to the Philippines, working abroad and remittances are recast as nationalist acts.

"Heroism," however, comes with responsibilities. While migrants are valorized as "heroes," the state also expects them to be exemplary representatives of the nation abroad. Workers are expected to be law-abiding, diligent workers who return to the Philippines once their employment visas expire. When workers fail in their nationalist duties, the Philippine state deploys numerous mechanisms to discipline them transnationally. Here migrant citizenship becomes a means by which the Philippines can, in fact, regulate migrants to obtain their remittances on the one hand and, on the other, intervene extraterritorially when migrants need to be brought under control since foreign states increasingly defer to the Philippine state as the appropriate custodian over unruly Philippine workers.

The Brokerage State and the Regulation of Global Labor Flows

While brokering labor serves the Philippine state's neoliberal imperatives domestically, it also performs the function of regulating flows of workers globally. As neoliberal globalization engenders new kinds of racialized and gendered labor demands, the Philippine state's system of labor brokerage enables the controlled flows of temporary workers across national borders, mobilizing them out of the Philippines and then ensuring their return back home. I would even suggest that labor brokerage might be a necessary institutional form (though problematic, especially for workers) under conditions of neoliberal globalization.

Neoliberal globalization is giving rise to the restructuring of labor markets and the reorganization of work and thereby creating structural demands for foreign migrant workers. Demands for foreign workers in the more economically privileged areas of the world system and prevailing inequalities between those areas and the periphery create the macrostructural conditions for international migration. Employers' ability to secure migrants is often mitigated by the resurgence of varieties of xenophobia and nationalism that are partly, it can be argued, a response to the new kinds of insecurities citizens of different countries around the world experience as a consequence of neoliberalism. In the face of precarious employment and dwindling social supports, many people are compelled to safeguard whatever limited entitlements their citizenship may offer under neoliberalism and call for immigration restrictions.

Regimes of labor brokerage, therefore, might offer a kind of institutional "fix" resolving global capital's demand for labor and neoliberalizing labor-importing states' demand for temporary migrants who will not make claims for membership and will return to their countries of origin once their jobs are done.[34] Labor brokerage systems can operate therefore at the convenience of global employers and host states. Employers need not assume liability for immigration law violations by employing "illegal" workers, yet they can still profit from wage differentials between native-born and foreign workers. They can, moreover, continue to exercise tremendous control over migrants whose legal status is attached to them. Employers are also able to take advantage of a temporary labor force that will not burden them with demands for wage increases or seniority benefits over time and is less likely to be organized by unions. They can, furthermore, benefit from the embodied labor of migrants, taking advantage of their bodily capacities for labor while they are yet in their physical prime. Labor-receiving states, meanwhile, can be assured a stock of temporary migrants who are tethered to their home countries and less likely to partake of government services.

International organizations like the World Bank (WB), the World Trade Organization (WTO), and the International Organization for Migration (IOM) have increasingly been championing guest worker programs (which systems of labor brokerage are) as the solution to the contradictions between global labor demand and immigration restriction. These organizations anticipate that guest worker programs will have:

> "win-win-win" outcomes, as migrant workers win by earning higher wages abroad, migrant-receiving countries win with additional workers who expand employment and economic output, and migrant-sending countries win via greater remittances and the return of workers who gained skills abroad. Workers often lose in the process.[35]

The Philippines is often held up as a "model" of "migration management,"[36] and there is in fact growing evidence that developing states around the world are engaging in their own kinds of "migration management" or what I call "labor brokerage" systems. Critically analyzing labor brokerage in the Philippines, therefore, becomes an urgent project, especially if we are concerned about what labor brokerage means for people's prospects to live and work with dignity and under conditions free from exploitation.[37]

The labor-sending state is perhaps the institution most able to effectively resolve the contradictory forces of labor demand and immigration restriction. It can perform regulatory functions that can be performed only by states. While private labor recruiters might be able to mobilize workers for overseas employers, they will ultimately confront state borders that may or may not permit migrants entry.[38] It is true that labor recruiters often move workers across these boundaries clandestinely; they may even produce fabricated documents to get past immigration authorities. Unauthorized migrations, however, pose too many challenges for labor-receiving states. They are forced to deal with multiple and contradictory domestic pressures from nativist groups, immigration rights advocates, and employers, as well as international pressures to conform to human rights conventions with respect to so-called "illegal immigrants." It becomes necessary for labor-receiving countries to identify alternatives to stringent immigration restrictions and the undocumented migrations they produce. Labor brokerage states may be precisely what labor-receiving states need to regulate global circuits of migrants as the labor-sending state has the authority to claim and the capacity to execute control over its population. States have "monopolized" the authority to legitimately control the movements of people across national borders.[39] It is with respect to the issue of national belonging and citizenship, on which this authority over border crossings rests, that labor-sending brokerage states are able to play a role in the global regulation of workers in a way nonstate actors simply cannot.

States continue to need to assert symbolically, if not actually, their sovereignty over their territory against encroachments from outsiders. Nowhere is the idea of open borders considered acceptable with respect to people. Yet given the global demands for workers, sovereignty may be taking new forms: "The scope of sovereignty is not essentially and in all respects tied to the territorial limits of states, and the way in which the exercise of sovereignty is related to territory can vary over time and place."[40] One way labor-receiving states may be able to secure their sovereignty in the face of international migration, undocumented and documented, may be to actually concede sovereignty to labor-sending states within the scope of their territory. That is, labor-receiving states can formally grant labor-sending states custodial power over their citizens. I would argue that the bilateral (and in some cases multilateral) negotiations that are increasingly vital to international transfers of labor are evidence of new configurations of sovereignty in labor-receiving and labor-sending states. One important bargain that is struck between these states is labor-receiving states' relinquishment of control over migrants to their home states, control that labor-sending states are only too eager to accept. This seems to be the model favored by groupings like the newly formed Global Forum on Migration and Development, for instance, which I will discuss in more detail in this book's conclusion. As Sassen correctly anticipates: "Reality has forced new conditions and new practices on the inter-state system. This contributes to the internationalization of the inter-state system and may well be an important precedent for handling other policy issues, including immigration, in a more multilateral manner."[41]

The international system of states sustains the national "difference" on which migrant labor systems, as a source of cheap workers for global capital, depend. Because systems of labor brokerage rely on the reification of national identities and citizenship, labor-sending states become ideal suppliers of workers for the world. As William Robinson suggests, "National boundaries are *not* barriers to transnational migration but are mechanisms functional for the supply of labor on a global scale and for the reproduction of the system."[42] Global capital continues to rely on national boundaries even as neoliberalism demands the diminishing of these boundaries. The unequal value ascribed to different forms of national labor, which is often rendered in racialized and gendered terms, is the means by which capital can extract surplus value from workers.

Book Overview

In chapter 1, I provide historical context for the emergence of labor brokerage in the Philippines. I suggest that the institutional precursors for contemporary labor brokerage can be traced to the colonial labor system established under the Americans at the turn of the twentieth century. Moreover, I argue that U.S. colonialism has had deep and lasting consequences for Philippine state formation and for the constitution of class relations in the Philippines well beyond formal national independence in 1946. Fundamentally a neocolonial state administered by elites long favored by the Philippines has been compliant with the U.S hegemonic neoliberal economic prescriptions. The government has introduced export-oriented development to at once sustain a social order favorable to domestic elite interests while maintaining the Philippine state's legitimacy in the global arena, where international recognition in the system of nation-states ultimately requires conformity to capitalist logics. Because neoliberalism has fundamentally destabilizing effects — effects that are significantly gendered — labor brokerage has become necessary to contain the social, political, and economic dislocations it produces. Labor brokerage became a practicable strategy for the government as international migration from the Philippines had already been normalized under the U.S. colonial administration. The Philippine state opportunistically took advantage of these historical legacies, on the one hand, and new forms of labor demand globally on the other in order to profit from the export of its citizens.

In chapters 2 and 3, I illustrate the specific mechanisms by which the Philippine state mobilizes workers for out-migration by examining the functions of the Philippines' transnational migration bureaucracy. I get at the "micropolitics" of power, those realms of state practice that often go overlooked and yet are essential to processes of globalization. I illustrate how the state has created education and training programs that are actually matched to the demands of labor markets around the world, which are monitored by the Philippines' global network of embassies and consular offices. I show how the state, moreover, uses its transnational apparatus to actively advertise Philippine migrants to overseas employers and to begin bargaining with foreign governments to facilitate their workers' out-migration. The state draws on racialized and gendered logics to pitch Philippine workers to foreign employers and governments (as Arroyo does above) as race and gender structure global demands for migrant labor. My discussions in this chapter draw from archival research of Philippine government documents, interviews with Philippine migration bureaucrats, ethnographic observations of the migration bureaucracy, as well as interviews with migrant workers themselves.

In chapter 4, I explore how the state has reconfigured meanings of nationalism and national belonging with respect to overseas migration, what I call migrant citizenship, to make the act of temporarily living and working abroad a commonsensical practice for ordinary people. The system of labor brokerage in the Philippines rests on a particular (one might dare say peculiar) sort of state–citizen relation. Under a regime of labor brokerage, Philippine nationalism is accomplished through one's departure from the nation-state. One is not, however, conscripted into military service, for instance. One is instead conscripted to serve as part of a reserve army of labor. State–citizen relations in the neocolonial, neoliberal Philippines is necessarily fragile, and it is therefore a site of persistent investment. The state engages in the active construction of citizenship through a myriad of practices. In this chapter, I am interested in its everyday bureaucratic practices as well as more formal policies. Bureaucracies and various kinds of bureaucratic practices are especially rich sites of study because it is in bureaucratic spaces and through both the banal and ostentatious practices of government that states and citizens encounter one another most intimately.[43] Hence, in addition to examining laws and other legal–juridical instruments to track shifts in citizenship, this chapter draws on ethnographic research, interviews with migration bureaucrats, and examinations of government documents produced and circulated within migration agencies.

The meanings of citizenship are often structured by gendered logics, as men and women figure very differently in the national imagination. Chapter 5 explores public debates about women's migration that plagued the Philippine state throughout the 1990s. As women's out-migration as domestic workers (as well as other gender-typed workers) began to outpace the out-migration of male migrants, public debates raged about whether the Philippines should either curtail or better regulate women's emigration. Nationalist anxieties were heightened by what was perceived as the "shame" women's out-migration as domestic workers brought to the Philippines' subject status globally. These anxieties fed into mass protests with the hanging of a Filipina domestic worker, Flor Contemplacion, by the Singaporean government in 1995. Protesters were outraged that the Philippine state did not prevent her execution. The transnational mobilizations, however, forced the Philippines to introduce new migration reforms manifested in the Act of 1995. In this chapter, I explore the gendered consequences these reforms had for understandings of nationalism and national belonging as they apply specifically to migrant women.

Chapter 6 focuses on the processes and outcomes of a wildcat strike where Philippine migrant workers employed in Brunei, exerting some of the very "rights" spelled out in the Migrant Workers and Overseas Filipinos Act, enlisted the assistance of Philippine state representatives to advocate on their behalf for higher wages and working conditions. Here I examine what migrant citizenship means for migrant workers and for the Philippine state in practice. On the one hand, the case demonstrates how the Philippine migrants often see their interests tied to and guaranteed by the Philippine state. On the other hand, as the outcome of the struggle reveals, though Philippine officials intervene on their citizens' behalf to some extent, they are willing to discipline those who threaten the Philippines' relations with foreign employers and host countries through forced repatriation and other sanctions.

In my concluding chapter I discuss the key insights my work on the Philippines offers to the scholarship on the state and international migration within the context of globalization. I then briefly describe emergent forms of labor brokerage outside the Philippines and suggest how my study here might inform future studies of this phenomenon. Finally, I discuss alternative meanings of rights and membership that migrant workers' groups like Migrante International offer. Migrant activists construct important visions of more equitable ways of being and belonging that become vital to consider in today's neoliberal global order.

1

The Emergence
of Labor Brokerage

U.S. Colonial Legacies in the Philippines

At Manila's Ninoy Aquino International Airport outbound airplanes
to Seoul, Rome, Kuala Lumpur, Doha, and Sydney depart daily filled
with thousands of migrant workers, men and women, young and old.
The taxis or colorful *jeepneys*[1] that make their way to the airport and
throughout the streets of Metro Manila are decorated with the names
and images of faraway destinations like "Saudi Arabia," "Japan," or
"San Francisco" as tribute to the migrants working in those places
whose remittances funded their purchase and operation. The drivers
of these very taxis or *jeepneys* are often themselves either waiting
for a new opportunity to work abroad or resettled in the Philippines
after having worked overseas. James Tyner describes Manila as a new
kind of "global city" as it is a critical locus for the out-migration of
contractualized workers for labor markets around the world.[2] Manila,
however, has long been linked to global labor circuits; as many Filipinos found themselves working first in Spanish[3] and then later in
U.S. colonial outposts including Acapulco, New Orleans, Honolulu,
San Francisco, and Seattle.

In this chapter, I situate the Philippine state's strategy of exporting labor within the historical context of U.S. colonialism in the
Philippines. The labor brokerage system in the Philippines is in large
part a result of the U.S. colonial legacy in the Philippines. First, it
is in the colonial labor system that we can track the institutional
precursors of this system. Second U.S. colonialism and subsequently,

*Figure 3. Ninoy Aquino International Airport's departure area, 2008.
Photograph by Ben Razon. Source: Sugar Mountain Media.*

neocolonialism has had deep and lasting consequences for the Philippines economically and politically. Neoliberalism in the Philippines today is a consequence of neocolonial structures.

Colonialism and International Migration: Filipinos as "Wards" and Workers

With the Spanish empire nearing its end in the final years of the nineteenth century, the United States primed itself to take over Spain's colonial outposts in Asia and the Caribbean. U.S. imperial designs led it to war with Spain, which ultimately resulted in the colonization of the Philippines, along with Puerto Rico and Cuba, in 1898.

The colonial subjugation of the Filipino people, however, was no easy task for the United States. It faced bitter resistance. Having been engaged in a fierce anticolonial struggle against the Spanish (this struggle played a role in weakening Spain's empire) that brought them to the brink of victory, the more radical elements among the Filipino anticolonial forces refused to kowtow to American military might. In what would become the Philippine-American War, Filipino anticolonialists waged a decade-long fight against the United States.[4]

Outgunned by the Americans, Filipino anticolonialists engaged in guerilla tactics to resist occupation. One scholar calls the Philippine–American war the "first Vietnam."[5] Frustrated by the Filipinos' unconventional martial tactics, the American military launched horrific campaigns of "pacification" that led to the torture and killing of civilians, including children. Pacification also meant the wholesale devastation of communities. Indeed, the "water cure," condemned most recently for its use by the U.S. military against detainees in Guantánamo Bay, was devised for and perfected first on Filipinos.[6] Those who survived these pacification campaigns were left without food, without water, without livestock, without land, without homes.[7] Conditions were such that many, when they were later given the opportunity to do so, would emigrate from the Philippines to the United States for employment.

There were those among the Philippine population, however, who were more than willing to collaborate with the Americans. Many of the economic elites from the Spanish colonial period, frustrated by Spain's refusal to allow them more political power, were more than eager to share power with the new colonialists.[8] Later, at the war's end and the establishment of civilian rule in the Philippines, they would be immediately incorporated into the colonial state apparatus. From their position at the helm of the government, their economic privileges could also be preserved. Ultimately both the political and economic structures set in place during the colonial period would be sustained even post-"independence."

While the Americans were consolidating their colonial state in the Philippines, the agriculture industry, particularly in the western part of the United States and in Hawaii, a newly acquired U.S. territory, was devising new strategies to secure cheap labor. Though agricultural employers had relied on low-wage workers from other Asian countries, including China and Japan, these groups proved to

be troublesome. Nativist U.S. workers threatened by the Asian workers spawned widespread anti-Asian violence, while Asian workers
became increasingly organized and militant. With the introduction
of the Chinese Exclusion Act of 1882 and the Gentlemen's Agreement of 1907, effectively cutting off these two key sources of labor,
recruiters soon looked to the Philippines. As a colony of the United
States, the Philippines became a convenient source of labor since Filipinos, considered "nationals" of the United States, were exempt from
immigration restrictions.[9] Labor recruiters actively sought laborers,
especially young men, from the Philippines. Representatives of the
Hawaiian Sugar Planters' Association (HSPA), for example, went to
the Philippines to secure workers. As Espiritu suggests, "because the
Philippines was a 'ward' of the United States from 1905 to 1935, the
[HSPA] could rely on the assistance of American colonial officials
there."[10] Employers would later hire labor contractors from among
Filipinos based in the United States to assist in recruiting friends and
relatives.[11]

In urban areas, meanwhile, Filipino men typically found jobs in
the service sector, for example, as "houseboys," chauffeurs, and hotel
workers.[12] This phenomenon anticipated the out-migration of Filipinos (both men and women) for employment in exactly these kinds
of jobs later in the century. By the 1930s, more than a hundred
thousand Filipinos were in the United States.[13]

The importing of Filipino workers became a means of addressing both the economic and the political imperatives of the United
States during this period. First, the colonial migrant labor system
could assure the United States of a continuous pool of cheap foreign labor. Moreover, because Filipinos were U.S. nationals, they did
not pose the kinds of political tensions for the U.S. government that
workers from other countries did.

While the ravages of the war on the one hand and the labor
demand in the United States on the other were important in shaping
the out-migration of low-skilled agricultural and service workers from
the Philippines, specific aspects of U.S. colonial rule in the Philippines
after the war also gave rise to other migratory streams.

With the increasingly successful suppression of the Philippine anti-colonial struggle by the end of the first decade of the twentieth century, the U.S. colonial state proceeded to transition from a military to a civilian occupation of the Philippines. Moreover, in order to consolidate its base, that is, its collaborators among the Philippine elite, the United States sought to incorporate them into the state apparatus. Through a process of "Filipinization" the elites would occupy the ranks of the government and civil service. As part of an emergent strategy of "benevolent assimilation" violent suppression would be less central than a more inclusive logic (though of course, this transition did not necessarily mean the end of the suppression of Filipinos — the new police forces would carry that out). To prepare Filipinos for the task of working in and for the government, the U.S. launched the *pensionado* program, recruiting the young, mainly sons of elite families, for training and education in American universities.

Benevolent assimilation also aimed at transforming the hearts and minds of ordinary Filipinos in the Philippines through education, what Renato Constantino calls the "miseducation" of the Filipino.[14] Where military garrisons were erected, alongside them or replacing them were schools. Elite *pensionados* made their way back to the Philippines and as the idea of the "American Dream" spread more widely among the population who were being educated under the new American system of education, more and more Filipinos would make their own way to the United States to further their education. As part of its new mission of "benevolence," the U.S. colonial state also expanded public health and encouraged the training of nurses in the United States. In many cases, education in the United States would create pools of "unintentional immigrants."[15] Ultimately, however education in the United States or the Philippines, whether specialized in nursing or governance or not, produced a kind of culture of migration among many Filipinos. As Filipino-American writer Carlos Bulosan described it in the title of his novel written during this period, "America is in the heart." Of course, Filipinos' colonial subject status as "nationals" enabled their entry into the United States as workers or students. The U.S. military also served as a conduit for migration as Filipinos were allowed to serve in the U.S. Navy, where they mainly worked as stewards to American naval personnel.[16]

The Beginnings of Brokerage

Several institutional precursors to the contemporary labor brokerage state can be identified in the colonial labor system, including the expansion of training programs, the role of labor recruiters, and the role of the state in facilitating out-migration.

One important initiative under the U.S. project of benevolent assimilation was the introduction of public health and therefore the training of nurses in the Philippines. According to Catherine Choy in her close study of the historical origins of nurse migration from the Philippines to the United States before nurse training programs were fully established in the country, prospective nurses, generally selected from the most elite families, were sent by the colonial government to the United States for training through the *pensionado* program in the first decade of the twentieth century. Like other *pensionados* sent to study in the United States under the program, Filipina women trained as nurses in American institutions returned to the Philippines to assume high-status positions in Philippine hospitals and their affiliated nursing schools. Over time, study in the United States came to be viewed by broader segments of the population as a sure path to upward mobility in the Philippines, and many more women attempted to find their own means of getting to the United States.

By the 1920s and 1930s, Americanized nursing education in the Philippines was put into place, and women did not necessarily have to leave the Philippines to get an American nursing education. Yet, as Cathering Choy argues, "Americanized nurse training established by the U.S. colonial government actually laid the groundwork for Filipina migration to the United States."[17] Though the Tydings–McDuffie Act of 1934 would put a halt to Philippine immigration to the United States, Filipina nurses would later find entry into the United States through the U.S. Exchange Visitor Program (EVP) in 1948.

The EVP was aimed at serving U.S. Cold War ideological aims by providing participants from abroad with the opportunity to work and study in U.S. institutions while also receiving a monthly stipend. It was hoped that the program could countermand anti-American sentiment propagated by the Soviet Union. The EVP was not aimed solely at exchanges of hospital personnel, nor was it a program geared toward strengthening Philippine–U.S. relations specifically. Yet by the 1960s a majority of the participants were from the Philippines, and of the Philippine participants, most were nurses. According to Choy, "Once Filipino nurses and the Philippine government became actively involved in the EVP, the Philippines began to dominate participation in the program."[18]

Arguably, the Philippine government's active participation in EVP laid the groundwork for the institutionalization of labor export in the early 1970s. The year before President Ferdinand Marcos formally introduced the labor export program through Presidential Decree (P.D. 442), he lauded the EVP program for helping Filipina women to secure jobs abroad.[19]

Some of the very same early twentieth-century programs would continue to train nurses (and then later, caregivers) for overseas employment at the turn of the twenty-first century. St. Luke's Medical Center, for instance, was established during the U.S. colonial period, and it was at St. Luke's where I observed a training program for prospective caregivers headed to Canada to work under their Live-In Caregiver Program in 2000–2001.[20]

The phenomenon of Philippine-based labor recruiters also finds its beginnings in the colonial period and the immediate postcolonial period. As mentioned earlier, the Hawaiian Sugar Planters' Association (HSPA) actively engaged in recruitment in the Philippines in the 1910s–1930s. Nursing recruitment agencies facilitated the transfers of nurses under the EVP in the late 1940s and then engaged in more aggressive recruitment when the program's residency requirements changed and new avenues for immigration were opened up with the 1965 U.S. immigration law.

The role of labor recruiters in facilitating Philippine workers' international migration during the colonial period and during the early

years of "independence" prefigures the emergence of the labor recruitment industry in the Philippines in the contemporary period. The
global deployment of Philippine workers today is due in part to the
work of recruiters in mobilizing Filipinos and Filipinas for employment
overseas.

As important as labor recruiters were (and continue to be) in facilitating immigration to the United States, they were limited in their
ability to operate since immigration legislation in the United States
would restrict migration from the Philippines until 1965. Ultimately,
the labor recruitment industry, while important to facilitating international labor flows, is confronted with barriers erected by states.
What would facilitate migration from the Philippines to the United
States, however, would be diplomatic relations between the two
countries.

As anti-Filipino sentiment spread in the United States, the U.S.
government was forced to curtail the immigration of Filipino workers through the Tydings–McDuffie Act of 1934, as I mentioned
above.[21] The act basically spelled out Congress's plan for the eventual
independence of the Philippines. With an independent Philippines,
Filipinos would no longer be U.S. nationals, and therefore Filipino
immigration could be effectively halted. Filipinos would no longer
be considered U.S. nationals, but Philippine citizens. They would
be considered "foreigners" and subject to entry restrictions. Filipino
immigration to the United States would be limited to a mere fifty
a year. Nevertheless, the U.S. government would also allow Filipina
women entry into the United States to study and work as nurses
through the EVP in spite of immigration restrictions spelled out in the
Tydings–McDuffie Act. Agreements secured between the U.S. government and the new Philippine government formalized the transfers
of Filipinas to the United States.

In addition, military agreements between the two countries provided Filipinos with continued opportunities to migrate, although
U.S. immigration law formally prohibited it. Even without U.S.
citizenship, Filipinos were allowed to serve in the U.S. armed forces
around the world, and they used the opportunity to get into the
United States.[22] Filipinos' participation in the U.S. military especially

the Navy, beginning in the 1950s in many ways marked the beginning of the globalization of Filipinos, perhaps too the beginnings of Filipinos' dominance as seafarers globally.

As migration through the EVP and the U.S. military reveal, labor transfers from the Philippines were possible during a period of severe immigration restrictions through agreements between the United States and the Philippines. The role of the Philippine state in formalizing labor flows to other countries through bilateral relations would later prove to play a decisive role in the globalization of Philippine workers.

As I discussed earlier, the Philippine state's institutionalization of out-migration through Presidential Decree 442 in 1974 came on the heels of its active promotion of the EVP program among Philippine nurses. This policy, however, would shift the locus of international migration from the United States, which had dominated earlier out-migration from the Philippines, to destinations around the world. The colonial labor system under the United States, including the introduction of training programs for overseas employment and the labor recruitment industry, would form the backbone of the contemporary migration apparatus. In the past, private actors played a role in the training and recruitment of migrant workers with minimal state interference, given the Philippines' status as a colony of the United States. However, under the Marcos government the state would engage in the processes of training and recruitment itself, while also regulating private actors to capitalize on out-migration as a means of generating foreign exchange.

The profitability of out-migration was already evident under the colonial administration. Philippine families had come to depend on their relatives' remittances from abroad for their sustenance. Moreover, the migrant labor system generated revenue for the colonial state since "the main rationale for these early statutory regulations under American colonial rule (1898–1946) was to take advantage of the high private sector demand for cheap labor from the Philippine Islands to raise much-needed revenue for the U.S. government's coffers."[23]

The need for the Philippine state to generate revenues and therefore institutionalize out-migration, however, is tied to the other
structural consequences of colonialism, namely, the distortion of the
Philippine economy and the sedimentation of earlier class formations in positions of political power. As I discuss in the next section,
these conditions of neocolonialism, which have enabled the fast-
tracking of neoliberalism in the Philippines, have given rise to labor
brokerage.

Neocolonialism and
Modern Philippine State Formation

The end of World War II marked the end of U.S. colonial rule in the
Philippines and, therefore, independence, by an act of the U.S. Congress in 1946. Though the act offered sovereignty to the Philippines,
that sovereignty was in fact incredibly limited. Specifically, the U.S.
government was able to maintain a great degree of political control
by securing positions of power for its erstwhile collaborators and the
installation of U.S. "advisors" as part of the newly formed government. Moreover, the United States maintained its military presence
in the Philippines as agreements forged between the two countries
would allow the Americans to retain military bases throughout the
archipelago.[24]

Moreover, U.S. firms were able to maintain their economic dominance through key provisions in the Philippine constitution. With
its preservation of U.S. economic and political interests, the newly
"independent" Philippine state was, in fact, a neocolonial one. U.S.
capital, for example, continued to be guaranteed by the Philippine
constitution in the "Parity Amendment":

> The disposition, exploitation, development, and utilization of all agricul-
> tural, timber, and mineral lands of the public domain, waters, minerals,
> coal, petroleum, and other mineral oils, all forces and sources of potential
> energy, and other natural resources of the Philippines, and the operation
> of public utilities, shall, if open to any person, be open to citizens of the
> United States and to all forms of business enterprise owned, controlled,
> directly or indirectly by United States citizens, except that the Philippines

shall not be required to comply with such part of the foregoing provisions of this sentence as are in conflict with such Constitution.[25]

To safeguard its economic interests in the Philippines the United States had to support a particular constellation of domestic class relations. Specifically, it created conditions such that landed families would continue to lord over Philippine society, which relied on age-old feudal relations.[26] This arrangement, however, would have disastrous consequences, as severe trade imbalances and economic crisis ensued through the 1950s. The Philippines' lack of technological development in agriculture as well as limited access to the once open U.S. market rendered it unable to successfully compete worldwide. The Philippine government, however, would turn to its erstwhile colonizer for both aid and advice. The aid they got was in the form of IMF loans, and the advice they received was to continue to keep the economy open to "free" trade.[27] The Philippines needed to be a bulwark against communism in the region. It "provided a test case of the benefits that might accrue to countries from having close friendships with the United States."[28] While the United States certainly had economic interests to maintain in the Philippines, it also had geopolitical interests in propping up the country in whatever way it could.

By the 1960s, however, there was some debate among economic and political elites in the Philippines about the future course of the economy. Some advocated more nationalist economic policies like import-substitution industrialization to protect their nascent industries, while others advocated a shift to export-oriented industrialization (EOI) that was ultimately compliant with U.S. advice. This debate, however, was cut short as Marcos broke the stalemate. With U.S. assent Marcos declared martial law in 1972 and set the economy onto a firm course of EOI.[29]

Marcos's economic program was fully in line with the dominant economic development paradigm advanced by global capital and multilateral institutions like the IMF and World Bank and, of course, U.S. interests.[30] Marcos's justification that his economic program required the declaration of martial law in 1972 to institute economic discipline was widely supported by the West.[31]

Neoliberalism and the Export of Labor

EOI, however, still left the Philippines struggling with balance of payment requirements and rising unemployment. President Marcos then institutionalized labor export with Presidential Decree 442, which created three state agencies, the Overseas Employment Development Board (OEDB), the Bureau of Employment Services (BES), and the National Seaman's Board (NSB). The OEDB, BES, and NSB were responsible for the development, promotion, regulation, and implementation of the labor export program. Two agencies, the OEDB and the NSB, were the government placement agencies for workers (recruiting and deploying land-based and sea-based workers respectively), while the BES was devoted to the regulation and supervision of private recruitment and placement agencies that were allowed to play a role in facilitating overseas employment as the state increasingly lacked the capacity to fully handle this aspect of migration.[32]

The Philippine state sought to capitalize on existing out-migration while also expanding it given new forms of labor demand globally because remittances migrants sent back to the Philippines proved to be economically beneficial. Migrants' remittances helped to strengthen the country's foreign exchange reserves and thereby help the government to maintain its debt repayments. Marcos violently suppressed the growing communist movement, which was at the forefront of the struggle to depose his dictatorship. He saw the export of labor as an important measure to curb the political unrest likely to be exacerbated by un- and underemployment.

The returns on overseas workers' remittances, however, could not fully alleviate the balance of payments crisis. The Marcos administration was forced to seek relief from the International Monetary Fund in the latter part of the 1970s, which imposed strict structural adjustment programs (SAPs) that only served to plunge the Philippine economy into further economic crisis. SAPs are neoliberal programs that require developing states to enact economic policies that foster free trade and an outward orientation.[33] Among the export-oriented strategies recommended by the IMF as a means of garnering foreign investment and ostensibly relieving the crisis were tourism and the expansion of light manufacturing (garments, electronic components, etc.). Both strategies, which continue to be crucial to the Philippine economy, are critically gendered as they require the labor of women. The Philippine state, for instance, enticed capital investment in Export Processing Zones (EPZs) with the labor of Filipina women, who were represented as an especially docile and cheap labor force. Filipina women were similarly used to attract foreign capital through tourism.[34] Rather than highlighting Filipinas' docility, the state promoted the "beauty and generosity of Filipino women as 'natural resources' to compete in the international tourism market." With its hosting of the Miss Universe pageant in 1972 the Philippines established itself as an exotic destination and a land of beautiful women.[35] The Philippines' labor export policy was instituted in the same year. Even as the government's export-oriented programs provided forms of employment for some people, SAPs ultimately meant increasing unemployment and decreasing wages for most.[36] The gendered tourism and segmentation that characterizes export-oriented employment confines women to low-paid, low-status jobs. Moreover, they suffer from unequal pay, which then becomes an inducement for out-migration.[37] With the maturation of the labor brokerage system it will export women workers to labor in tourism and manufacturing overseas.

By the 1980s the Philippines was one of the most structurally adjusted in the world. By 1983, the total foreign debt was $42.8 billion. Not surprisingly, that same year Marcos mandated that remittances be sent through the Philippine banking system with Executive Order 857. Workers would be subject to punitive measures if they failed to remit their earnings. Through the end of the 1980s, the Philippines became even more dependent on foreign loans as trade imbalances and increasing debt forced it to seek even more aid from the IMF as well as loans from private lenders. These loans were attached with yet more stringent conditions. The economy was not helped, of course, by Marcos's notorious corruption.[38] Even though overseas employment could not fully absorb the dislocations wrought by neoliberal economic policies mandated by SAPs, it continued to be actively promoted by the Philippine state. In addition to making remittances mandatory, in 1983 it consolidated existing migration agencies to form the Philippine Overseas Employment Administration (POEA).

The year 1986 marked what many believed would be the beginning of an era of renewal and promise for the Philippines with the fall of the Marcos dictatorship and the rise of Corazon Aquino. Swept into the presidency by the massive "People's Power Revolution," Aquino manifested the return of democracy and the possibility for economic recovery, yet little changed. Aquino inherited the economy left by her predecessor, and she assured creditors that even with the transition, the Philippines would make good on its debts. By 1988, debt service was $3 billion or 37 percent of the national budget. By 1989, debt service consumed 44 percent of the budget. Moreover, it was clear that her government would keep the Philippines on the path of neoliberalism.

Though overseas employment was supposed to have been a temporary measure, it took on an increasing permanence as the neoliberalism that characterized the Marcos regime was carried forward by subsequent presidents. Hedman and Sidel argue:

> The "People Power Revolution" appears less as an example of the spontaneous resurgence of civil society in the process of transition from authoritarian rule and more as the climax in a cycle of recurring crisis and temporary "resolution" stemming from deep-rooted tensions in the underlying structures of Philippine democracy that have yet to be resolved.[39]

The "underlying structures" they refer to include sets of class and political relations ultimately rooted in colonialism that continue to persist despite regime change from dictatorship to democracy. Ben Reid argues:

> Economic policy in the Philippines was almost completely confined to a strictly neoclassical framework. The kernel of policy emphasised the need to focus on the Philippines' purported comparative advantage in agriculture and as such both reflected and added to the hegemony of land-owning and rentier capital in the Philippines.[40]

Feudal relations have virtually persisted to this day. Though democracy and notions of "participatory development" emerged during this period, Reid further argues that "each political regime after Marcos was based on nearly identical national political and social interests; they have all embraced internationally sponsored neo-liberal restructuring and liberalization."[41]

Moreover, military violence against ordinary people did not wane with the fall of the Marcos dictatorship. Though hers was considered a democratic regime, Corazon Aquino nevertheless pledged in front of the U.S. Congress that she was committed to "total war" against those who might stand in the way of her instituting the economic and political mandates required of neoliberalism. This campaign of total war included the massacre of peasant activists who rallied in front of the presidential palace demanding genuine land reform. Total war was ultimately necessary for the Philippines to continue to implement neoliberal economic policies and to coerce the Filipino people into accepting them. At the same time, those who could be mobilized for overseas employment were siphoned away from the country and inserted into global labor markets. Of course, given the difficulty of everyday life, many went overseas willingly. The temporary fix that Marcos had initially anticipated for the labor export program came to take on more permanence.

President Fidel Ramos, who succeeded Aquino, can perhaps be considered the most ambitious in terms of implementing neoliberal reform. His Medium Term Philippine Development Program (MTPDP), alternately called "Philippines 2000," was to lay the groundwork for the Philippines' fast track to NIC-hood. Despite some economic growth from trade liberalization, for ordinary Filipinos life is still difficult, for the Philippines' perennial unemployment has not been alleviated.[42] During an interview a high-ranking official in the Philippines' migration bureaucracy concurred: "The issue becomes one of sustainable growth. Economic growth alone does not equal jobs. Globalization does not always result in the same kinds of jobs because of contractualization and flexibility." This was certainly true during the Ramos years.

Alongside the aggressive implementation of neoliberal economic reform, the Ramos presidency paved the way for the remilitarization of the Philippines by the United States through the Status of Forces Agreement (SOFA), which has evolved into the Visiting Forces Agreement (VFA), an executive agreement that resurrects many of the provisions contained in the U.S.–Philippine Military Bases Agreement of 1947. Moreover, joint Philippine–U.S. military exercises were resumed under the Ramos presidency. It seemed that for neoliberalism in the Philippines the strong arm of the Philippine police and military no longer sufficed; rather it required the muscle of the U.S. military.

In addition to these economic, political, and military developments, Ramos continued to actively promote international migration. Overseas employment had become an important means through which the Philippine state contained the social dislocations that neoliberal economic development policies engender. Under his administration, the POEA issued a white paper that asserted that the communist insurgency was quelled by international migration. In other words, if militarization cannot sufficiently quell the communist movement, migration can.

The promotion of migration is increasingly the way beleaguered Philippine administrations attempt to address political crises. During the height of the political and concomitant economic upheaval that plagued the Philippines in late 2000 when President Joseph "Erap" Estrada was impeached by the Philippine House of Representatives for graft and corruption, the Department of Labor and Employment (DOLE) issued a statement noting that "overseas employment would continue to sustain, if not save the economy from collapsing this year."[43] In the wake of Estrada's toppling in what came to be termed "People Power 2," the newly inaugurated President Gloria Macapagal-Arroyo included migration as a component of the nation's recovery program. The newly appointed DOLE secretary released a statement not long after President Arroyo's rise to power asking migrant workers to "invest their earnings in the Philippines to hasten economic recovery and help the country regain lost ground."[44] However, like her predecessors, Arroyo has no qualms about violently eliminating those who oppose her.[45]

Conclusion

The ravages of the Philippine–American war, the restructuring of Philippine society under U.S. colonialism, along with labor demand in the United States, produced the structural conditions for large-scale emigration from the Philippines to the United States. However, other institutional arrangements under the colonial labor system established by the Americans would ultimately serve as precursors to today's labor brokerage system. For instance, while the establishment of the public education system by the Americans played a role in shaping Filipinos' imaginaries about the United States and undoubtedly influenced people to seek opportunities to emigrate, the establishment of training programs for specific occupations like nursing at the turn of the twentieth century would become instrumental in facilitating the emigration of nurses from the Philippines. These early training programs prefigured the vast complex of training programs geared toward global labor markets that comprise a key aspect of labor brokerage today. Arguably too, the role of labor recruiters in securing short-term contractual employment for Philippine workers under the American colonial administration is likely to have normalized that form of employment which would be among the defining features of labor brokerage post-"independence." Finally, the state-to-state relations that organized transfers of labor from the Philippines to the United States (despite the introduction of major immigration restrictions at the conclusion of formal colonization) would foreshadow the informal and formal diplomatic relations that regulate labor flows under a system of labor brokerage in the contemporary moment.

Just as significantly, the economic, political, and social structures that were established in the Philippines under U.S. colonial domination laid the basis for neocolonial conditions post-"independence." The so-called "independence" of the Philippines hinged on the consolidation of the Philippine economic elite at the government's helm.

The elite were ensured their status and wealth in exchange for concessions to U.S. economic, political, and military interests that were folded into the Philippine constitution as well as passed early on by Philippine legislators. The logics of free trade and export-orientated development, two pillars of neoliberal orthodoxy that underlie contemporary economic policy in the Philippines, sustain these earlier formations and make employment overseas a vital means of survival for many ordinary Filipinos.

The Philippine government has attempted to monopolize emigration for its own ends by institutionalizing a program of labor export and mechanisms aimed at capturing migrants' remittances. At the same time, overseas employment absorbs potential political strife.

2

A Global Enterprise of Labor
Mobilizing Migrants for Export

Philippine migrant workers are practically everywhere. Wherever I have traveled, internationally and within the United States, I always encounter workers from the Philippines. When in Madrid as part of an international Philippine studies conference, I came across a Filipina caregiver walking with a young Spanish child. Interestingly enough, it was during a tour of the stomping grounds of Philippine anticolonial nationalist writer José Rizal. In South Africa during a vacation with my family in Cape Town I observed hundreds of Filipino seafarers enjoying, like us, a beautiful day at the Victoria and Albert Waterfront. When I checked in to my hotel for the Midwest Sociological Society's annual meeting in Omaha, Nebraska, the woman helping me at the front desk was a Filipina.

Filipinos and Filipinas work in countries as varied (and perhaps unexpected) as the United Kingdom, Norway, Azerbaijan, mainland China, Canada, Australia, and even Gabon (see Figure 4).

Though I am a Filipina, my own travels are enabled by my highly coveted blue American passport as well as by my position as a U.S.-based academic. I can hardly recall a time that I have had difficulty entering any country of my choice. Moreover, I can travel visa-free to many parts of the world. Most Philippine migrants, however, possess neither highly privileged passports nor professional status. Philippine citizens generally need to confront directly the immigration authorities of the countries where they hope to be employed as soon as they deplane or disembark from ships sailing international waters. As an archipelago of over seven thousand islands in Southeast Asia, the

Region	Number
Middle East	393,654
Asia	253,276
Europe	51,970
Americas	11,258
Africa	9,098
Trust Territories	7,595
Oceania	2,859
Unspecified	4,260
Total Land-based	733,970
Total Sea-based	247,707
Total	981,677

Figure 4. Destinations for Overseas Filipino Workers, 2005. Source: POEA.

Philippines does not share land borders with neighboring countries; migrants can therefore leave the Philippines only by plane or ship. Philippine passport holders will be expected to present their passports and evidence of entry authorization in the form of a visa. They can rarely enjoy international travel (for pleasure let alone for work) without some kind of restriction, unlike passport holders from the West (like me) or wealthier economies like South Korea or Singapore. Pei-Chia Lan notes that "the passport, a tag of membership bestowed by the state of origin, is also a document of personhood required for one's entrance into and circulation in the global labor market."[1] Perhaps more than the passport, a visa is necessary for temporary employment overseas as "visa restrictions on passport holders from certain countries are one of the most important mechanisms with which nation states exert their prerogative to control entry into their territory."[2] Visa requirements may include training verifications, health screening, and police clearances that are to be completed prior to departure. The question then is how is it possible for Philippine workers to be as globally mobile as they are?

In this chapter, I argue that the global scope and scale of Philippine migration is enabled by the transnational bureaucracy the Philippine

Figure 5. Manila's Mall of Asia, 2008. Photograph by Ben Razon. Source: Sugar Mountain Media.

government has developed as a means of mobilizing migrants for export. The government agencies responsible for facilitating out-migration perform the function of "authorization," that is, training and documentary processing, which together allow aspiring migrants to leave the Philippines for jobs overseas.

As Pierre Bourdieu suggests, the state possesses the power of "authorization," through which it produces "socially guaranteed identities (as citizen, legal resident, voter, taxpayer, parent, property owner)."[3] Capital and goods can flow relatively freely across borders, but the transnational flow of people continues to be highly circumscribed. States are especially careful about who is and who is not permitted to cross their borders. As Cunningham and Heyman observe, "borders permit, monitor, and halt movement. The notion of movement then needs to be seen within the context of mobilities enjoined with enclosures."[4]

Migrants' mobility is possible only if it is "authorized." In other words, migrants are mobile only when they possess passports and the appropriate visas necessary to enter another country. Philippine labor migrants' ability to cross hundreds of borders for work every day depends on migrant-receiving states' (and foreign employers') recognition of the authoritative power of the Philippine state. For instance, only the Philippine state can legitimate its citizens' membership and eligibility to travel through the issuance of a Philippine passport, which is bestowed only on those who can establish their national identities as Filipinos with official birth certificates and who can prove their travel worthiness with police clearances. Moreover, migrant-receiving states issue employment visas only after evaluating certifications of prospective migrants' previous employment, education, or training. They cannot rely solely on the certifications granted by migrants' former employers or schools; rather, they rely on the Philippine state to affirm that the documents submitted by prospective migrants are in fact valid. "Our ontological security sometimes needs to be endorsed by bureaucratic and juridical apparatus, which is when state documentation such as the passport and the visa is considered of high truth value. In this light, passports and visas, by signifying one's legal status in an official document, provide the institutional foundation of trust during international or transnational encounters."[5]

International migration, in other words, relies on relations of trust between nation-states secured through processes of "authorization" performed in large part by labor-sending states' bureaucracies. These bureaucracies are especially important sites for study because it is through mundane practices like documentary processing that labor-sending states exercise their authoritative power and facilitate the border crossings of migrants. Yet too often these practices are overlooked in studies of international migration. Certainly the migration industry and migrant networks play an important role in facilitating out-migration. Ultimately, however, the authorization practices of labor-sending states' bureaucracies are crucial to border crossings around the world.

"Authorized" migration requires that the Philippine government be closely attuned to the specific visa categories for temporary workers that exist in different countries around the world and ensure that prospective migrants conform to them. I will detail how the state gathers this information and describe the mechanisms by which the Philippine government mobilizes migrants for these jobs through, first, market-driven skills and training programs and finally through documentary processing. Through this analysis of the government's migration bureaucracy I illustrate how the labor-sending state is indispensable to international migration of Philippine workers. However, I will also provide an "on the ground" perspective that discusses migrants' experiences as they negotiate the bureaucracy to secure overseas employment.

Immigration Intelligence

Though many countries around the world have introduced restrictive immigration policies, they have not eliminated immigration outright. Instead, they might limit foreign workers to employment in specific job categories or industries or regulate migrants' entry through stringent documentary requirements. As immigration scholars have shown, different receiving countries around the world have enacted policies that aim to serve employers' needs for labor while also placating citizens' fears that immigrants are taking away their jobs. The Philippine state, however, is able to effectively mobilize its citizens for overseas work by carefully studying the nuances of a variety of immigration regimes and then preparing migrants to comply with the restrictions defined by these regimes so they can secure employment abroad.

The Philippine Overseas Employment Administration (POEA) and the International Labor Affairs Service (ILAS) play important roles in monitoring trends in labor demand globally, paying close attention to immigration policies. Based in the Philippines, the POEA as one official describes it is "an LMI [Labor Market Information] institution, generating various statistical and qualitative data that deal with the temporary migration or contract employment of Filipino human resources around the globe." The POEA has a Marketing Branch that serves the function of "monitoring...different labor markets. We examine what the policies are for foreign workers in various countries and make recommendations about what Philippine policy should be for a specific market. All markets are monitored." The POEA's Marketing Branch has regional desk officers for nearly every area of the world including Asia, the Americas, the Middle East, Europe, and Africa. The POEA coordinates closely with ILAS, which has representatives in the Philippines' embassies and consular offices around the world (Figure 6). As of 2007, ILAS had thirty-four Philippine Overseas Labor Offices (POLOs) staffed with "labor attachés" in Asia, the Middle East, the Americas, and Europe. A top-ranking official of ILAS explained that "labor attaches help with marketing by being the eyes and ears in foreign labor markets. New policies that may affect foreign labor are studied."

The Philippines' diplomatic corps contributes to market research by identifying labor market trends and ultimately initiating discussions with host countries to help facilitate Philippine workers' entry into specific labor markets, as I will detail in the next chapter. The establishment of formal diplomatic relations through the establishment of embassies and consular offices in particular countries is often linked to the presence of a market for Filipino labor (Figure 7).

Migration agencies actively circulate information about new immigration policies as a means of mobilizing Philippine workers for overseas employment by producing "Market Updates," which are advertised at government agencies and circulated in the news media. Additionally similar kinds of alerts are posted on the POEA's website.[6] "Market Updates" contain information generated by ILAS's POLO offices throughout the world as well as by embassy and consular offices that are referred back to Philippine-based migration agencies. These agencies then reconcile these data with the information that has been collected from international media and even foreign embassies based in the Philippines. Figure 8 focuses on those Market Updates collected during my field research in 2000–2001 that specifically discuss migration policy in labor-receiving countries.

Middle East	Asia and the Pacific
Abu Dhabi, United Arab Emirates	Bandar Seri Bagawan, Brunei
Al Khobar, Saudi Arabia	Hong Kong, China
Beirut, Lebanon	Kaohsiung City, Taiwan
Dubai, United Arab Emirates	Kuala Lumpur, Malaysia
Iraq (operating from the	Macau, China
Philippine embassy in Kuwait)	Osaka, Japan
Jeddah, Saudi Arabia	Seoul, South Korea
Kuwait	Singapore
Manama, Bahrain	Taichung City, Taiwan
Oman	Taipei, Taiwan
Qatar	Tokyo, Japan
Riyadh, Saudi Arabia	
Tel Aviv, Israel	*Europe*
Tripoli, Libya	Athens, Greece
	Geneva, Switzerland
Americas and	London, England
Trust Territories	Madrid, Spain
Saipan, CNMI	Milan, Italy
Toronto, Canada	Rome, Italy
Washington, D.C., United States	The Hague, The Netherlands

Figure 6. *International Labor Affairs Service (ILAS) offices, 2007.*
Source: ILAS.

It offers a good illustration of the sorts of "market" information produced by the various Philippine migration agencies both in the Philippines and overseas. It is important to note that the migration officials responsible for doing market research pay attention to a range of countries. These range from industrialized countries that have been countries of immigration like the United Kingdom and the United States to newly industrializing countries like Malaysia and even the Isle of Man, "an internally self-governing dependent territory of the Crown which is not part of the United Kingdom."[7] The data in Figure 8 indicate that the employers of migrants include

Abuja, Nigeria
Amman, Jordan
Ankara, Turkey
Athens, Greece
Baghdad, Iraq
Bandar Seri Begawan, Brunei
Bangkok, Thailand
Beijing, China
Beirut, Lebanon
Berlin, Germany
Berne, Switzerland
Brasilia, Brazil
Brussels, Belgium
Bucharest, Romania
Budapest, Hungary
Buenos Aires, Argentina
Cairo, Egypt
Canberra, Australia
Caracas, Venezuela
Dhaka, Bangladesh
Dili, East Timor
Doha, Qatar
Hanoi, Vietnam
Havana, Cuba
Holy See (Vatican)
Islamabad, Pakistan
Jakarta, Indonesia
Koror, Palau
Kuala Lumpur, Malaysia
London, England

Madrid, Spain
Manama, Bahrain
Mexico City, Mexico
Moscow, Russia
Muscat, Oman
Nairobi, Kenya
New Delhi, India
Ottawa, Canada
Paris, France
Phnom Penh, Cambodia
Port Moresby, Papua New Guinea
Prague, Czech Republic
Pretoria, South Africa
Riyadh, Saudi Arabia
Rome, Italy
Safat, Kuwait
Santiago, Chile
Seoul, South Korea
Singapore
Stockholm, Sweden
Tehran, Iran
Tel-Aviv, Israel
The Hague, The Netherlands
Tokyo, Japan
Tripoli, Libya
Vienna, Austria
Vientiane, Laos
Washington, D.C., USA
Wellington, New Zealand
Yangon, Myanmar

Figure 7. Philippine embassies, 2007. Source: Department of Foreign Affairs.

families seeking domestic workers (Malaysia). They also include hospitals and other medical facilities, public and private (United States, U.K., and Kuwait). The information and communications technologies industry (United States, Switzerland, U.K., and Germany) as well as agriculture (Malaysia) also secure workers from overseas. In addition to looking at new migration policies favoring foreign workers, the Philippines' market research analyzes political developments in different countries to anticipate potential migration policy changes that might lead to opportunities for employment. In other words, migration functionaries even try to make projections about labor market trends. These projections become important, as I detail in the next chapter, because countries with prospective employment visa availabilities are targeted for informal and formal "labor diplomacy" by the Philippine state.

The market logic that shapes the orientation of Philippine officials and government agencies toward overseas employment reveals the extent to which Philippine citizens have become reduced to mere commodities to be bartered and traded globally. The Philippine state is implicated in placing its citizens in low-wage, low-status, temporary jobs around the world. Most labor-importing countries typically set aside the most undesirable jobs for foreigners. As a labor broker the Philippine state gives over its citizens' livelihoods to the vagaries of global labor markets even as it expects them to support their loved ones who themselves are subject to the precariousness of everyday life under conditions of neoliberal globalization in the Philippines.

Defined by a logic of what David Harvey calls "flexible accumulation," global capital has given rise to radical transformations in the labor markets globally. He argues:

> Faced with strong market volatility, heightened competition, and narrowing profit margins, employers have taken advantage of weakened union power and the pools of surplus (unemployed or underemployed) labourers to push for much more flexible work regimes and labor contracts.... More important has been the apparent move away from regular employment towards increasing reliance *upon part-time, temporary or sub-contracted work arrangements.* [emphasis added][8]

Country, Year	Employment visas
Kuwait, 1999	"The Philippine Overseas Labor Office in Kuwait reported the following developments in the hiring of nurses of the Ministry of Health (MOH): The MOH shall employ private manpower agencies to hire and manage nurses at the MOH effective year 2000.... The MOH contract is for two years and renewable."
United States, 1999	"The Nursing Relief for Disadvantaged Act (H.R. 441) was signed into law by President Clinton on 12 November 1999. The law has created a new category of visas, H-1C to be used to place foreign nurses to work in areas designated as 'Health Professional Shortage Areas.' "H-1C nurses can be admitted for a period of three (3) years, and no extensions are provided." "Up to 200 H-1C visas are available to be issued each year."
United States, 1999	"A proposal for a new visa category which would allow U.S. companies to hire foreign workers to fill the nearly 350,000 vacant positions in the informational technology field was introduced."
Malaysia, 2000	"The Malaysian government lifted its ban on the recruitment of foreign workers in plantation, labor intensive industries and household workers effective 28 February 2000."
Switzerland, 2000	"According to the Philippine embassy in Berne, the business sector in Switzerland has proposed that the market for computer specialists be open to foreign workers to alleviate the shortage and meet the growing demands of the telecommunications and electronic commerce sectors in the country."
Isle of Man, 2000	"Midwives from the Philippines could be deployed to the Isle of Man to work in nursing homes as nursing aides or health care practitioners provide they have the proper work permits issued by the Department of Trade and Industry, Overseas Labour Section, Isle of Man Government."
Germany, 2000	"The German Cabinet recently approved two regulations governing the employment and residence status of foreign information technology (IT) specialists.... Both regulations will take effect from 01 August 2000 to 31 July 2008."
United Kingdom, 2000	"The Overseas Labour Service of the Department of Education and Employment in the United Kingdom announced that the hiring of midwives, physiotherapists, and Information Technology specialists is now open for non-European Union countries. These professions are designated as shortage occupation."

Figure 8. Employment visas in POEA market updates, 1999–2000.
Source: POEA.

It is precisely these developments that the Philippine state seeks to take advantage of. An official from the POEA's Marketing Branch, for instance, describes how the U.S. information technology (IT) industry is a viable market for Philippine migrants while the Canadian IT industry is not: "This industry hires temporary workers. It is a market for Filipino workers. Unlike the Canadian IT industry, which favors immigrants, there is no prospective market there."

Of course, since countries of immigration like the United States, Canada, the United Kingdom, and Australia have made it more and more difficult for people to immigrate and settle as legal permanent residents, temporary work sojourns may be the only way people from the Philippines can enjoy employment in these places. Most other countries have very restrictive immigration regimes anyway. For the Philippines to profit from the brokerage of labor, it needs to be fully cognizant of the modes of entry that do exist for job-seeking Filipino and Filipina citizens. And it is. The Market Updates listed in Figure 8 provide further evidence of the Philippines' interest in supplying temporary labor to countries that have historically been destinations for more permanent emigration from the Philippines. A 1999 Market Update for the United States details then-President Clinton's introduction of the H1C visa, a temporary, nonrenewable, three-year visa. The H1C actually offers nurses the opportunity to secure legal permanent residence but only upon the sponsorship of their employers. Migrants can be subject to extreme forms of exploitation under these kinds of conditions as employers may use the promise of sponsorship to squeeze as much as they can from workers in those three years. Studies of the Live-In Caregiver Program in Canada which operates through the same logic, have proven just as much.[9]

The Philippine state's marketing research is not limited to identifying immigration policy openings; it is also attentive to immigration policy closures. To maintain positive relations with labor-receiving countries the Philippines must regulate out-migration by discouraging migrants from attempting to seek employment in those countries that have imposed limits on employment visas. Figure 9, like Figure 8, draws on data I collected while conducting field research in the Philippines in 2000–2001. While Figure 8 examines those Market Updates that detail available and potential employment visas that Philippine migrants can apply for to get jobs overseas, Figure 9 looks at immigration restrictions and exclusions. For instance, a Market Update for Jordon and Bahrain describes how these governments are moving toward the nationalization of employment and thereby eliminating jobs for foreigners. Market Updates for other countries like the U.K., Spain, and Israel clarify erroneous information about visa availabilities presumably to prevent would-be migrants from attempting to apply for specific kinds of jobs in those countries. Finally, there are Market Updates that provide details on new restrictions imposed by labor-receiving governments that either limit migrants' residency (CNMI) especially if they are unemployed (Italy) as well as new penalties or sanctions imposed on employers who hire migrants (Israel).

Visa regimes both reflect and reproduce globalized hierarchies between nation-states. People bearing passports from some countries (generally non-Western, peripheral states) are less likely to be granted visas than others. At the same time, these national hierarchies become a means by which employers justify the unequal treatment of specific nationalities of workers. Indeed, national differences are often racialized. Rochelle Ball, for instance, documents how in Saudi Arabia nurses are recruited according to a racialized division of labor with Americans and Europeans favored for more supervisory hospital positions (for example, head nurses), while Filipinas and Egyptians are designated to work in subordinate positions. Ball suggests that

> nurses, like other contract workers, are recruited and paid according to an international hierarchy of jobs and conditions of employment; more powerful and skilled positions are more readily available to workers from developed nations. The conditions of employment and extent of personal freedom vary by nationality, and by the relative wealth of sending nations.[10]

If employers can use globalized hierarchies to generate profits by paying differently racialized workers unequal wages, the Philippine state

Country, Year	Immigration Restrictions
Israel, 1999	"The Israeli Minister of Interior does not issue working visas to Filipino workers in any sector other than the caregiving profession."
Bahrain, 1999	"Bahrain is in the lead among the Gulf States in replacing expatriate workers with their nationals in the public sector according to a survey conducted by the Economic and Social Committee for West Asia."
Jordan, 1999	"The Jordanian government, through the Ministry of Labor, is persistently pursuing activities that give preferences to Jordanians in line with the national government's campaign to address the rise in unemployment."
Syria, 1999	Syria "only allows foreign technicians to work in multinational firms and oil companies operating in Damascus and some other parts of the country. Other categories of workers such as domestic helpers, hotel, and medical staffs are not permitted to work in the said country."
Commonwealth of the Northern Marianas Islands, 1999	"Governor Pedro P. Tenorio signed into law Public Law No. 11-69 popularly referred to as the three-year stay limit for nonresident workers."
Spain, 1999	"The Spanish Ministry of Labor denied reports that the Spanish government will allow the entry of 300,000 immigrants to relieve its labor shortage in the field of agriculture and construction."
Israel, 2000	"The Knesset Finance Committee in Israel recently approved a new law that will make it less attractive for Israeli employers to hire expatriate workers, excluding Palestinians."
Italy, 2000	"The Permit of Stay will no longer be extended nor renewed if a foreigner has been absent from Italy for more than six months except for serious reasons." "An unemployed foreigner is allowed to be enrolled only for one year in the Lisa di Collocamento (Employment List) in order to obtain another employment with work contract. If the foreigner remains unemployed after one year, his Permit of Stay will no longer be renewed and he shall be expelled from Italy."
U.K., 2000	"The Philippine Embassy in London emphasized that there is no opening for Filipino midwives in the U.K."

Figure 9. Immigration restrictions in POEA market updates, 1999–2000.
Source: POEA.

stands to profit from these very hierarchies. The promise of earnings in foreign currencies stronger than the Philippine peso, however
temporarily, becomes a draw for prospective migrants even if it slots
them into lower-paying jobs relative to native workers. Meanwhile,
when workers' wages make their way back to the Philippines, the
state is able to strengthen its foreign currency reserves and thereby
pay its numerous debts.

Training Philippine Labor

To complement its research on immigration policies in different
migrant-receiving countries, Philippine migration agencies also train
prospective Philippine migrants to comply with specific skill requirements attached to different visa categories. According to a POEA
official, market research is also about reforming migration policy for
"manpower development." "Manpower" is developed through skills
training.

The Philippine state ensures that migrants are provided with
plenty of opportunities for skills training through the Technical
Education and Skills Development Authority, or TESDA. Though
TESDA's mandate is not limited to training workers for overseas
employment (it is supposed to train Philippine workers for the
national labor market as well),[11] TESDA is, nevertheless, engaged
in training Philippine workers for employment abroad:

> TESDA takes responsibility for the provision of relevant, high quality
> technical education and skills development supportive of the needs of
> enterprises and the country's goals through enabling policies, respon-
> sive programs, and quality standards. TESDA integrates and orches-
> trates multi-sectoral and market-oriented efforts among its stakehold-
> ers to respond to the changing demands of the domestic and global
> environments.[12]

Skills training complements the Philippines' public education system where instruction is conducted often in English. Philippine
workers' ability to speak English has long been a draw for foreign
employers.[13] While the Philippine government does provide technical education and skills training directly, the education and training

offered through TESDA is actually done through private facilities. The state sets parameters for these facilities and licenses only those institutions that exhibit the capacity to address global labor demand.

Prospective migrants are often required to provide evidence of skills training to secure employment visas from host governments. Though they may already have work experience that matches their hoped-for overseas job, they are still required to provide certification of competency in particular sets of skills. In either case, prospective migrants will seek training or certification from TESDA institutions. Ed was a college graduate with a degree in architecture in his early thirties. He was hired to work as an interior designer for a Saudi Arabian company. Ed explains: "I had to take a trade test at the Santa Ana Philippine Trade Testing Center because I needed to get certification. This was just a formality, but all technical workers have to do this."

While he describes the completion of the test as a "formality," Ed also believes that he benefits from the certification process. He states, "We need to send people in a professional manner; that's why the trade test is good. . . . We're good workers, so it's good to expand employment overseas, but we should show professionalism. We need a classification system so people won't be exploited." For him, trade training and testing is a means by which the state helps to professionalize migrants. Professionalization, for Ed, gives people better opportunities for work because it ostensibly protects workers from exploitation. Skills training or "upgrading" and "professionalization," however, cannot fully protect workers from exploitation. Even in the United States, often figured in Philippine migrants' imaginations as the ideal country of destination (it is, after all, a "nation of immigrants"), professional workers are subject to harsh living and working conditions. The Filipino immigrant press as well as the venerable *New York Times* reported how one group of nurses from the Philippines based in New York received wages far below federal standards, were overworked, and were subject to terrible living conditions as some were forced to sleep on the floor in an overcrowded and frigid apartment. In a cruel twist of fate, these nurses were then indicted by the Suffolk County district attorney's office on charges

Figure 10. Seafarers in training, 2008. Photograph by Ben Razon.
Source: Sugar Mountain Media.

of patient negligence when the nurses finally decided to walk out on
their employers.[14]

Prospective migrants are actually expected to pay for training
themselves. Rather than seeing training as protection from exploitation, some workers see it as a form of exploitation by the government.
Mike complained that training programs are just "money-making
ventures. The government and the centers are in cahoots! The government just makes it harder for us. It doesn't do anything for us.
They're just milking us. . . . We're 'heroes,' we've saved the economy,
but what's their help for us?" The grassroots transnational migrant
workers' organization Migrante International actually protested in
front of the Philippine government's office in Hong Kong on International Women's Day in 2007 against a mandatory training program
for domestic workers. Though the program is aimed at "profession-
alizing" the domestic workers, activists claim that it is really meant

to fatten government coffers. The burdensome debts that migrants accrue from the training centers, private labor recruitment agencies, or banks to finance the costs of training (as well as other costs associated with securing overseas employment including documentary processing fees and airline tickets) can serve as a mechanism for disciplining workers. As I learned in my interviews with workers, lenders make arrangements with employers to have migrants' wages siphoned off to pay for these debts. Employers then turn around to offer migrants "incentives" for earning "extra" money. Often migrants end up working overtime and for less pay.

An astounding number of TESDA-certified courses are offered throughout the country. Numbering in the thousands, there are TESDA-certified training institutions to be found in each of the Philippines' fifteen regions. In the National Capital Region, by far the most populated region in the Philippines, the two largest cities of Manila and Quezon City proliferate with TESDA-certified training centers.[15]

These institutions offer a vast range of courses. The most numerous includes computer secretarial; computer technician; cosmetology; electronics technician; hair and beauty; mechanics (automotive and diesel); security guard; and tailoring and dressmaking. Other courses include: dental technician; health aide; pharmacy aide; care giving; computer-based bookkeeping; food and beverage services; baking and pastry arts; hotel housekeeping; industrial electrical technician; telecommunications technician; basic machine operation; industrial sewing; machine shop practice; welding; and a range of computer-related courses from computer applications to computer programming. Using the "market research" discussed above (Figure 8), the employment visa categories identified for 1999 and 2000 included, for instance, jobs in the areas of information technology, nursing and other medical personnel, and domestic workers. Comparing TESDA course offerings with the labor demand identified in this market research shows a clear match.

Immigration policies, insofar as they define specific visa categories for particular kinds of work in response to domestic labor demands,

Table 1. Overseas Filipino Workers (OFWs)
deployment per skill and sex, 2006

Occupations	Men	Women
Administrative and managerial workers	528	289
Agricultural, animal husbandry, and forestry workers; fishermen and hunters	716	91
Clerical and related workers	3,271	4,640
Production and related workers, transport, equipment operators, and laborers	80,240	23,338
Professional, technical, and related workers	17,212	24,042
Sales workers	2,405	3,111
Service workers	16,135	128,160
Total deployment by sex	120,507	183,671

Source: POEA.

reflect gendered logics. Examining the actual deployments of Filipino and Filipina workers, we see clear evidence of this (Table 1).

Jobs in the categories of "Clerical and related workers," "Sales workers," and "Service workers," which include jobs like receptionists, shop assistants and demonstrators, domestic workers, and caregivers, which are typically typed as "female" jobs, have, in fact, been filled by Filipina women. Men predominantly work in the category of "Production and related workers, transport, equipment operators, and laborers"; it is notable that garment workers, which are classified under this category, are mainly women. Meanwhile, women dominate in "Professional, technical, and related workers" because the jobs of "entertainer" and "nurse," which both fall under this category, are generally typed as work that women do.

Though none of the immigration policies profiled by the Philippine state's market reports in Figure 8 explicitly designate visas for men or women, understandings about which gendered bodies are most appropriate for and suited to specific types of work ultimately underlie them.[16] Chang and Ling argue that global restructuring "valorizes all those norms and practices usually associated with Western capitalist masculinity." Masculinized globalization is another process of global restructuring that "concentrates on the low-wage, low-skilled menial service provided by mostly female migrant workers."[17] Certainly, as indicated by Table 1, women work in clerical jobs and service jobs where they likely have to cater to the business and leisure needs of male professional workers.

Immigration policies are additionally shaped by racializing logics. These logics can work in contradictory ways. In some contexts these racializing logics restrict foreign workers to "3D" jobs (dirty, dangerous, difficult), while in others they may favor foreign workers who exhibit putatively positive attributes and are considered more Westernized, civilized, and desirable as English-speakers.

Some forms of labor demand, like the demand for maids, are sometimes less about securing a worker's labor power and more about reproducing the "female employer's status (middle-class, non-laborer, clean) in contrast to herself (worker, degraded, dirty)."[18] The status that the female employer and even her family members assume is a racialized (typically "white") one. The labor brokerage state, therefore, participates in reproducing unequal racial orders in supplying middle-class and elite families around the world with Filipina domestic workers.

While TESDA training is aimed at providing prospective Philippine migrants with specific skills commensurate with the demands of global labor markets as they are defined by different countries' visa restrictions, at the same time Philippine migration officials believe that it must invest in workers' training in order to maintain Filipinos' competitiveness over other nationalities of migrant workers. In 2001, the secretary of labor declared that the Philippines enjoyed the advantage of being an English-speaking country (thanks to U.S. colonialism). But to maintain its advantage globally it would need to continue "promoting and sustaining investments in the education and training of Filipino workers." By upgrading the skills of workers, it is believed, the Philippine state is better poised to capture a greater share of the global labor markets. One official notes, "The Philippines is attempting to create a niche in skilled labor." Arguably, the Philippine state stands to profit even more from skilled workers as they ostensibly are paid higher wages and are therefore able to remit greater amounts of money.

My ethnographic research of various TESDA-certified programs, though limited since my research was primarily focused on state institutions, affirm the findings of other Philippine migration scholars that employment agencies along with training programs work to mold women to become domestics.[19] I found, for instance, that TESDA training attempts to ready poor women for employment in more affluent households overseas by teaching them the basics in household appliance operation; many do not own the labor-saving technologies that can be found in middle-class households in wealthier economies. They are also given cooking instructions on local cuisine. The training administrator for a caregiver course believed that part of her task was to discipline doctors to "live in humility" in order to prepare them to work in lower-status jobs as caregivers.

Furthermore, TESDA-certified programs, though privately owned and operated, support the Philippine state's efforts in encouraging prospective migrants to maintain their linkages to the homeland by supporting their relatives in the Philippines or by directly funding state developmental initiatives. Without any prompting on my part, the administrator for the caregiver program, for instance, described how she merely wanted to "help the Philippines." Specifically, she was concerned with the fact that many Filipina women were leaving the country to work as "entertainers." She explained, "I felt bad for the Japayukis;[20] that's why I was interested in introducing this course. I think we need to equip them with skills." She hopes that the training program will not only provide women with skills but also that it will instill nationalism. "We need to teach them. Filipino values

need to be improved." Anna Guevarra's study of the recruitment
and training of Filipina nurses finds that the Philippine state engages
in strategic partnerships with employment agencies through which
what she calls an "ethos of labor migration" is intensified.[21] My own
research confirms her findings.

Documentary Processing

Documentary processing is perhaps the most important function of
the migration bureaucracy. Through the bureaucracy, migrants' documents are verified to meet the requirements defined by different
countries. Those whose dossiers are incomplete are instructed on
what to do to be in full compliance with specific national migration
regimes. Moreover, migrants' employment contracts are evaluated for
their conformity to the Philippine government's standard employment contract, which was established ostensibly as a protective
measure for migrants. The sense of security that the contract certification process is meant to give workers, as I will show in chapter 6,
merely serves to mask the fundamentally flawed and ultimately anti-
worker logic that actually organizes the Philippine government's
employment contract standards.

The very spatial organization of each of the key nodes of the migration bureaucracy is structured for maximum efficiency. Migrants are
processed through each agency in a remarkably orderly way despite
the volume of people handled on a daily basis. The ordered operations at these agencies are in sharp contrast to the disorder and chaos
that characterize the operations of all other governmentally regulated
aspects of Philippine economic, political, and social life. Just outside
the POEA compound, for instance, one is confronted with unruly
Manila traffic: road markers and traffic signs have no meaning and
are blatantly disregarded as a matter of habit. Yet the POEA manages
to process thousands of people for overseas employment every day.
In 2007 alone, the POEA processed a total of 1,077,623 migrants.
This averages about 2,952 daily.[22]

Though the space of the bureaucracy is already highly rationalized
and efficient, bureaucrats are constantly engaged in trying to better

Figure 11. Prospective migrants awaiting processing at the POEA.
Photograph by Ben Razon. Source: Sugar Mountain Media.

organize bureaucratic space to speed up bureaucratic processing. In 2000 the Department of Labor and Employment (DOLE), which oversees the POEA, launched a "Continuing Service Improvement" project aimed at institutionalizing "productivity and service quality improvement, " according to a POEA bureaucrat. As part of DOLE's project, the POEA committed itself "to improve service delivery by being recognized and certified by the ISO [International Organization for Standardization]. The ISO is evaluating how we conduct our operations. Already the sea-based center has an ISO award because it reduced what was once an eight-hour process to only three hours. DOLE wants to win a quality management award and to be the first in government to receive such an honor." The POEA even penalizes private employment agencies that fail to deploy workers within sixty days of contract certification. This is a dramatic reduction from the previous requirement of 120 days.[23] When I returned to the Philippines in 2008, I learned that the POEA achieved the goal of ISO certification.

The rational and efficient organization of the POEA, evidenced in its spatial organization and state officials' efforts to better rationalize its space, illustrates how the state is invested in the production of migrants for export. The more rational and efficient operations of the migration bureaucracy allow for the speedy processing of contractual laborers for global deployment, laborers who have increasingly become a profitable commodity for the Philippine state. At the same time, the rapidity with which bureaucratic processing is completed means that an employer can secure Philippine labor with great facility. Sociologists of development might argue that the rationalization of the bureaucracy points to the Philippine state's developmental capacity in labor export.[24] The bureaucracy operates like a well-oiled machine facilitating the process of authorization and thereby expediently speeding up the export of labor. Philippine migration scholar Maruja Asis suggests that the POEA "has made it easier for foreign employers or principals to obtain workers from the Philippines."[25] Arguably too, initiatives like the ISO certification, based on actual achievements in the migration bureaucracy, serve as a badge of honor that the Philippine state can use as proof in the international arena and at home that it is far from being "backward" and can stand side by side with other "modern" states.

From the perspective of prospective migrants, however, documentary processing is an onerous task; many spend several days going from government office to government office to secure the paperwork they need to leave for overseas work. The costs of documentary processing can be quite expensive as the Philippine government charges prospective migrants a fee for each of the documents they need.

Ryan sarcastically describes how "the only thing that goes fast is paying fees. That's the fastest, paying fees, but the processing takes long." Even before Migrante International's protests against the fees associated with mandatory training programs, it long championed a campaign against what it calls "state exactions." In 2007 the POEA generated 346.1 million pesos from documentary processing fees. These "state exactions" as I mention earlier can serve to discipline workers in new ways. Migrants are forced to work all the more slavishly to pay off debts they incur to pay government processing fees and the other costs of securing overseas employment.

Though it is true that the spatial organization of migration offices like the POEA is ordered in a way that rationalizes migrants' documentary processing, it is also true that the space is closely policed. There is a highly visible presence of security guards in all of the Philippines migration agencies. At the POEA, guards are posted on every floor, in the stairwells, and in front of each of the different sets of service windows. They direct the flow of bodies through the building, making certain people are situated at the appropriate service windows and stay in their places in the queues. Guards often verify would-be migrants' documentation before they move from one set of service windows to another, and they even prevent people from moving on if they deem their documents to be incomplete. I found that the policing by security guards intimidated migrants. As I would try to approach people for a possible interview, I was brusquely brushed off or ignored. People were afraid that engaging in any activity outside of the prescribed purpose of the space would threaten their chance at overseas employment. One young woman fearfully queried, "You're sure you won't give my information to them [the POEA]? This won't affect my application, will it?" One effect of this surveillance, I would suggest, is to underscore the vital importance of authorization among migrant hopefuls. In some ways the monitoring that takes place in the Philippine migration agencies serves as a rehearsal for what is likely to be even more stringent examination at international borders. This becomes yet another mechanism by which the Philippine state can guarantee foreign states a properly authorized labor force that abides with immigration strictures, and perhaps it is also a way that the state can deliver employer-clients a labor force that is compliant as well.

Authorizing International Migration

The experiences of prospective migrant workers reveal how training is critically linked to the issue of authorization. Daisy, a single woman in her late twenties, failed to secure factory employment in Taiwan though she had hoped that her sister or her brother-in-law, who were already employed in Taiwan for several years, would be able to get her a job. Desperate to join them, Daisy applied to work as a domestic worker through a private recruitment agency. She believed, rightfully, that she would easily be able to get a job as a domestic worker, given the high demand for domestic workers in Taiwan. Prior to leaving, Daisy took a monthlong TESDA-certified training program for prospective domestic workers, which taught her how to operate various household appliances, cook basic Taiwanese dishes, and speak key phrases. She was diligent about attending the classes, in part because she did not want to face any difficulties in securing her work visa. One of Daisy's friends was denied an employment visa as a sales clerk in Taiwan because it was discovered that she had falsified her employment resume. According to Daisy, "At least they [Taiwanese immigration authorities] can't question my skills because I am getting trained."

Pei-Chia Lan holds that migrant workers contend with a "bounded global market"; that is, in spite of high degrees of economic integration and high demands for foreign labor, Asian states "impose a series of legal, political, and economic regulations on migrant contract workers."[26] The Taiwanese government has, for instance, set low ceilings on the entry of unskilled foreign workers, though it is generally liberal in its acceptance of higher skilled professional workers. Given the quotas on lower-skilled workers, Taiwanese employers often attempt to bribe local officials to grant additional quotas in order to secure foreign labor. Even if employers desire cheap workers from abroad, they depend on their government to grant those workers entry. Daisy's strategy of earning a skill through a state-regulated training facility makes sense as her mobility is circumscribed by specific sets of immigration restrictions in Taiwan.

Labor-receiving governments, meanwhile, entrust only labor-sending states with the ability to guarantee that the individuals they are sending have met their requirements. An application form for authorization to work in Taiwan, for instance, indicates that "the worker and the deployment manpower agency should sign this document in person at the office of the labor authority of the labor-sending country for authentication," which in the Philippines would be the POEA. There are consequences for those who fail to have it appropriately signed. "This authenticated document should be handed to the employer in Taiwan for purposes of processing workers' work permit. Failure to present this document would mean refusal of issuance of Work Permit by the Council of Labor Affairs, Executive Yuan, Republic of China, and would result in the repatriation of the foreigner according to the regulation."

Chiari and Lorenzo, a husband and wife with a young son, were undergoing training together as caregivers when I interviewed them. Chiari was actually a practicing dentist, while her husband Lorenzo ran a small car wash from their home. Both of them saw the caregiver training course as a chance for them to secure work in the United States through a relative who owned a care home in California. They had applied for tourist visas to the United States twice before, but were denied. Chiari described how difficult the interview process was at the U.S. embassy: "They ask you a lot of questions, but you can't explain your answers in Tagalog, only English. I don't think we gave good answers when we were interviewed before. We hope this will be a good avenue for migration because my uncle handled our H1B visa papers since we're going to work for him."

Chiari believed that after completing the caregiver training course and receiving their certificates, they would be able to better handle the interview process at the U.S. embassy. "At least when we are finished with this course we will get a certificate. When they interrogate us at [U.S.] immigration, we can prove to them that we're really interested in working there. We don't have to fake it because we'll have the certificate." She noted, "We could never go to the U.S. embassy without the certificate that we have graduated. They get so suspicious." Lorenzo joked, "You can actually buy a [fake] certificate. But if they ask you at the embassy if you understand this course that you finished, then it is good to complete it anyway." Training and the successful securing of job offers are not sufficient for migrant workers to be able to work overseas. Crossing borders for employment requires that migrants also secure visas from their host states.

In my interviews, I found that authorization from countries like the United States as well as other industrialized countries like Canada or the European countries can act as a guarantee for prospective migrants seeking jobs in any country around the world. A.J., a private English tutor in South Korea, recalls how her father, a retired construction worker who spent most of his working life in Saudi Arabia, had all of his children visit him in Saudi Arabia and helped them to travel and visit relatives in other parts of the world while they were young so that they could accumulate tourist visas from many different countries. He believed that his children's record of travel (so long as they did not violate the provisions of their tourist visas) would eventually help them to apply for overseas work once they were adults. A.J., along with most of her siblings, was able to secure tourist visas for countries in Europe and for the United States. She believed that her previous travel experience and accumulated tourist visas did in fact help her when she decided to work abroad.

An examination of the visa application requirements for South Korea reveals that A.J. may have been partially correct in her assumptions: the South Korean government exempts "holders of valid visas to the U.S.A., Canada, Japan, Australia, and New Zealand" from applying in person at the South Korean embassy in the Philippines.[27]

My cousin Peter's case also illustrates how authorization from key states like the United States is seen by migrants as opening up opportunities for other forms of migration. Peter was hired to work as a manager for a U.S.-based restaurant chain, which sent him for training in Los Angeles. That restaurant chain did not renew his contract, but eventually he got employment at another U.S.-based chain. He hoped that working for this chain would again allow him an opportunity to be trained in the United States or (the best case scenario) be transferred to work, even temporarily, in the United States. He was unable to renew his contract yet again and was left with a very narrow set of employment options in the Philippines. Peter was a casualty of labor flexibilization policies in the Philippine domestic labor market, which has led to increasing contractualization.[28] Both his U.S.-based employers required employees to sign waivers preventing them from

working in similar kinds of enterprises to safeguard against the leak-
age, he said, of "trade secrets." Overseas employment seemed to be
his only option for a job. Reflecting on his experiences with U.S.
employers, however, Peter believed that securing a job abroad would
not be difficult:

> Since I went to the United States for training and I came back to the
> Philippines when it ended, I think I can prove to other countries that I
> can be a responsible worker, that I'm not going to overstay my visa. When
> I was in the States, your dad joked that I should just TNT[29] because there
> are a lot of Filipinos who do that, but I couldn't. If I was a TNT I would
> be separated from my family for too long. Anyway, at least I can apply
> for a visa somewhere else. Also, since I worked for U.S. companies, I can
> prove that I have good skills.

Trixie's experiences offer a different vantage point for understanding the importance of authorization. Before settling into a job as a
beautician in the Philippines, Trixie had worked for many years in the
personal service of a Saudi Arabian princess. She described how she
had the opportunity to travel to the United States and throughout
Europe accompanying her employer on her family's private jet.

> The problem was the princess was too conniving. Since they had a private
> jet, they somehow managed to get past immigration. But because of that
> none of my trips abroad are reflected in my passport. Now that I don't
> work for her, I don't think I will have the same kind of opportunity to
> work abroad.

Throughout our conversation, I could sense Trixie's acute sense of
loss. At thirty-seven she was unmarried and without children since
she had spent so many years abroad. Continued employment overseas, she explained, might have offered her a sense of fulfillment,
allowing her to continue to support her younger siblings. But Trixie
felt that because she did not have records documenting her travel it
would be difficult to find another job abroad.

While the passport is an embodiment of an individual's national
citizenship, it is also a mode through which migrant workers' rights
are policed and delimited once they actually gain entry into another
country for employment. It is frequently the passport, a migrant's

Figure 12. POEA office, Mandaluyong City. Photograph by Ben Razon. Source: Sugar Mountain Media.

primary form of personal identification, that foreign authorities examine to ascertain whether migrants can have access to public space to engage in leisurely activities and whether they can settle and marry locals. One's national origin even impacts whether one will be allowed to or restricted from participating in labor unions or other kinds of organizations. Finally, as I suggest earlier in this chapter, the ascription of national identities onto particular working bodies is important for employers in many places as nationality becomes a means of assigning differential and unequal value (and therefore wages) to different sets of workers. As Aristide Zolberg suggests, "international borders serve to maintain global inequality."[30]

Finally, it is through the authorization process that migrants frequently become acutely aware of themselves as bodies of labor. A.J., for instance, expressed a sense of consciousness about her age and her health during the course of our discussion, the significance of which I could not initially grasp. She explained, "I work really hard 'cause I'm strong now. I have to take care of my body." Later, when I interviewed Mike, it became clearer to me why her health was so important to her. Mike explained, "Our only security is our bodies. If you fail a medical exam, it's the end of your profession. Even here if you are sick, you still have a job. But not abroad.... Who'll help us? We have nothing because we're contractual. That's where we lose." On the one hand, Mike's comments illustrate the gravity of authorization processes, including routine medical exams. Migrants' employment overseas requires that they be able-bodied persons (how "able-bodied" gets defined by foreign governments may be highly variable as age and other factors may go into its definition). At the same time, Mike's fears about getting ill also reflect the downside of contractualized work. Even as Mike may be able to earn better wages abroad, in the end he has no health or disability insurance that could help him in a time of need. Perhaps more tragically, these workers' sense of their bodies' diminishing capacities for labor over time illustrates how the logics of labor "flexibility," or, more aptly, labor "disposability" works: " 'disposability' turns on a calculation that measures the worth of discrete bodily functions,"[31] Migrant workers are only valuable (and therefore employable) inasmuch as they are useful and productive laboring bodies. Otherwise, they become mere waste that employers and states (both receiving and sending) can easily discard and replace.

Conclusion

Together the migration agencies that comprise the migration bureaucracy facilitate migration. The Philippines' migration agencies are able to assess global labor market demands by identifying visa categories specifically geared toward importing foreign workers. Meanwhile, the state's migration agencies perform the "authorizing" practices on which the global mobility of labor depends. These "authorizing" practices include the Philippine state's ability to certify prospective migrants' preparedness for specific occupations through skills training and assessment programs offered by the Technical Education and Skills Development Authority (TESDA), to corroborate an overseas job applicant's moral character through police clearances from the National Bureau of Investigation (NBI), and to authenticate the official membership and travel worthiness of its citizens with the issuance of a Philippine passport from the Department of Foreign Affairs (DFA). Evidence from migrants undergoing bureaucratic processing illustrates the crucial importance of the state's bureaucratic work in facilitating migration.

3

Able Minds, Able Hands
Marketing Philippine Workers

Photographs depicting Philippine workers employed as professionals, medical workers, operations and maintenance workers, construction workers, hotel workers, and seafarers are scattered throughout a glossy brochure entitled "Filipino Workers: Moving the World Today" produced by the POEA's Marketing Branch.[1] The text of the brochure, meant for distribution to prospective employers and host governments, describes the unique characteristics Philippine workers bring to various jobs. For example, it describes how Filipino professionals are:

> equipped with extensive educational training and a natural ability to adapt to different work cultures. They are ideally suited in any multi-racial working environment given a facility with the English language. Their professional competence earned for them the respect of their Asian and Western counterparts, making them much sought after in today's dynamic businesses.

In another part of the same brochure, the POEA lauds Filipino operations and maintenance workers. They have

> created a niche for their characteristic ingenuity, innovative spirit, skill, and dexterity. Through constant training and retraining they have kept themselves abreast with the latest technology. They benefit from a government-sponsored technical and vocational program that instills not only skills development but the right attitude towards work.

This brochure reflects logics similar to those evoked by President Gloria Macapagal-Arroyo's speech to American businesspeople in 2003, which opens this book. As in Arroyo's address, the POEA's

Figure 13. Brochure produced by the Philippine Overseas Employment Administration.

brochure refers to the training and education that the government provides. With respect to Filipino professionals specifically, the
brochure assures prospective employers and host governments that
they can be readily inserted into multiracial social orders triangulated
between presumably white (or even Asian or Arab) employers and
other racialized groups.[2] Similarly, Arroyo's pitch implicitly draws on
racialized discourses to represent the Philippine workers as modern
and civilized (in her terms "educated" and "English-speaking") and
therefore suitable for employment in any working environment. In
terms of blue-collar workers, the brochure promises its hoped for
clients workers who possess innate, essentialized characteristics like
"dexterity." Moreover, it guarantees that workers' training not only
sharpens their skills, but instills in them the "right attitude toward
work." As the previous chapter illustrates, the "right attitude toward
work" often means acquiescence and obedience.

Marketing materials such as this demonstrate that racializations of
Filipino migrants are not limited to the peculiar ways their host countries interpolate them into their specific (and in some cases emergent)
racial orders or how firms draw on racialized and gendered understandings in their hiring practices. Here the labor brokerage state
plays its own role in racializing and gendering Filipinos in particular
ways. Racializations of Philippine professionals, for instance, resonate
with the notion of the "model minority" often ascribed to Filipinos
and other Asian Americans in the U.S. context.[3] Meanwhile, the
racialization of manufacturing workers draws from the same sorts
of "capitalist scripts" used by employers in racializing Third World
women workers throughout the global South. These scripts try to
normalize women from the global South as an enduringly and endem-
ically cheap labor force.[4] As Juanita Elias describes in her research
of multinational firms' recruitment practices, recruiters have a strong
preference for women garment workers because "men were viewed as
unsuited to sewing work because they were easily bored and lacked
the manual dexterity 'nimble fingers' of women."[5] As performed by
the Philippine state, these scripts reproduce what Wright calls the
"myth of the disposable third world woman."[6] The state assures
employers that disposable Philippine workers, women (and men), can

nevertheless be quickly and easily replenished by a reserve army of Philippine labor at the ready for deployment around the world.

This brochure is but one example of how the Philippine state actively markets Filipina and Filipino workers to employers around the world. As I demonstrated in the previous chapter, the migration bureaucracy is a key site for the mobilization of migrant workers. Through agencies like the POEA, TESDA, and others, the Philippine government identifies where visas are available for temporary workers in countries around the world and provides potential migrants with the training necessary to get official authorization for those visas. Perhaps more importantly, it is through this apparatus that the Philippine state is able to actually formalize the transfers of Philippine workers globally. It is this distributive aspect of the migration apparatus, that is, the mechanisms by which the state actually exports workers for the world, that is the focus on this chapter.

Whereas the previous chapter illustrates how the state trains Philippine migrant workers in ways that match the requirements of labor-importing states' immigration policies, this chapter examines how the Philippine government actively works to *open up* markets for Philippine workers. I show, for instance, how Philippine migration officials closely monitor the economic and political trends and transformations wrought by neoliberal globalization in different societies of the world and how they then attempt to exploit potential opportunities for exporting workers through so-called "market promotions." I show how the state deploys techniques used in commercial advertising, like producing the above-mentioned brochure, to virtually "sell" Filipino and Filipina laborers to what migration officials refer to as "clients" (that is, foreign employers). Finally, I illustrate how the Philippine state engages in diplomatic negotiations with labor-receiving countries to formalize transfers of labor. Ultimately, Philippine labor's global mobility depends not only on labor demand, but on host states' willingness to open their borders to foreign workers. The Philippine state actually initiates different kinds of formal and informal relations with foreign governments to ensure out-migration.

Though there is certainly a thriving private labor recruitment industry in the Philippines, very few can compete with the state. No privately owned labor recruitment agency has the capacity to map global labor market trends in the way the Philippine government can, equipped as it is with a global apparatus of embassy and consular offices as I describe in the previous chapter. Private-recruitment agencies, therefore, cannot perform the same kinds of "market promotions" for Philippine workers that the state is able to. Neither can most agencies negotiate with foreign states around the issue of migration policy. If anything, recruitment agencies depend on the state's work in opening up markets for workers (even as the state itself profits from more and more migrants sending remittances home).

Markets for Migrants

The migration bureaucracy mobilizes Philippine citizens for overseas work through market research that identifies key labor migration policies in different countries and creates training programs to train prospective migrants in skills specified by these policies, as I describe in the previous chapter. In this next section, I analyze how the Philippine state's market research also pays attention to the trajectories of global capital's expansion and related economic developments in different countries in order to engage in more proactive measures to formalize outflows of Philippine workers to ever-new sites.

If the expanding U.S. military is identified as a potential market for Philippine labor, as evidenced in the introductory chapter, U.S. firms' global "commodity chains" are also prime markets for Philippine labor.[7] I learned during an interview with the Philippine government's labor attaché working from the Philippines' embassy in Brunei, for instance:

> [There are] new markets for Filipino workers in the garments industry because it is expanding. Brunei has an open quota to the United States — they can export finished garment products without a quota.

This was true at least in 2001 when I interviewed him. The factories I visited were producing garments mainly for U.S.-based retailers like the Gap and Old Navy, while the workers making the clothing were all foreign migrants, a majority from the Philippines. Because local Bruneians shun factory work and the Brunei economy depends on a diversification of exports for growth, Filipino and Filipina migrants can be assured of jobs in Brunei's garment industry according to this official. According to a Brunei-based labor recruiter who has worked throughout Southeast Asia supplying garment factories with low-wage workers, "When [a clothing tag] says 'Made in Brunei,' or 'Made in Indonesia,' it should really say, 'Made by Filipinos.'"

The most recent market reports posted by the POEA — which draws from research conducted by its own Marketing Branch as well as ILAS and Philippine embassies and consular offices abroad — provide additional evidence to suggest that both the U.S. military and U.S. capital and its global subsidiaries are important markets for Philippine labor. For instance, the U.S. Marines' relocation to Guam is identified as a potential source of jobs for Philippine migrants in a report posted in 2007: "The Philippine Consulate General in Agana, Guam has reported on the possible employment for OFWs in Guam on the U.S. Marines relocation project from Okinawa to Guam, which will start in 2010."[8] Of course the Philippines' long-time "special relationship" with the United States has made the U.S. military an important "client" for the Philippines for nearly sixty years.[9]

Meanwhile, reports for Canada suggest that the establishment of subsidiaries of major multinationals like Microsoft and Google are also potential markets for Philippine labor. This report explains that Microsoft's planned move to Canada is aimed at evading restrictive immigration policies in the United States and taking advantage of Canada's more liberal immigration regime:

> This announcement follows the recent "death" of the immigration bill that would have expanded the number of foreign high-tech workers that could enter the U.S. each year on H-1B visas. High-tech companies have been pushing hard for Congress to increase the number of visas they are allotted. Microsoft Chairman Bill Gates made a strong plea for unlimited H-1B visas while Google called for expanded ability to hire foreigners, which it credits for the company's success.

Meanwhile, Carnival cruise lines' joint venture with a Spanish firm also offers promising job prospects for Philippine seafarers.[10] Beyond Carnival, the Philippines generally dominates the international seafarers labor force.[11] While multinational U.S. firms around the world are a significant market for Philippine labor globally, even small and medium-sized enterprises (SMEs) can be important. According to an ILAS official, "There are so many prospects for Filipino workers so the focus must be on the bigger enterprises. SMEs can't be avoided, however, because it is often they who more immediately require foreign workers." SMEs in Asia, a major site for the employment of Philippine migrants, are often linked to U.S. multinationals. The Brunei factory I described above is an example of an SME linked to a U.S. multinational corporation. U.S. global capitalist restructuring has created specific dynamics in Asian newly industrializing countries (NICs). Though they have benefited from this restructuring, they continue to be dominated by the interests of capital in the core and are therefore vulnerable to its interests. Odekon argues, for instance:

> As neoliberal policies reshape and transform the semiperiphery economies and subject them more and more to the will of global capital in the core, the semiperiphery faces the danger of becoming a periphery. This prospect inevitably threatens the semiperiphery and, in particular, labor in the semiperiphery, which now faces similar marginalization in flexible labor markets.[12]

Consequently, NICs have turned toward the importation of unskilled or semiskilled workers to labor along those nodes of global commodity chains (like garments) that are located in their countries to perform "3D" jobs (dirty, dangerous, difficult) that locals have begun to shun. Importing workers is a measure to keep foreign capital investments flowing while simultaneously benefiting domestic firms.[13]

The Philippines markets the same types of labor it has supplied global capital even before the institutionalization of labor export. In chapter 1, I discussed how the Philippines supplied service workers ("houseboys," chauffers, and hotel workers), seafarers (for the navy) and nurses (though not intentionally) to the United States during the colonial period. Later, as I also discuss in that chapter, the Philippines' developmentalist initiatives in the decades immediately following "independence" would attempt to attract employers in tourism and light manufacturing. Now it actively markets these very categories of worker throughout the world. In the POEA's 2007 market reports, for instance, tourism-related jobs are identified in Singapore, Brunei, and throughout the Gulf States. Meanwhile factory jobs are identified in Taiwan and South Korea.

In spite of the national anxieties that the migration of Filipinas as domestic workers has produced in the Philippines,[14] the Philippine state works to actively locate markets for them.[15] In a 1999 labor market report, Israel was classified as an "emerging market" for domestic workers. Meanwhile, a 2004 "Market Update" for Hong Kong noted that it will continue to be a strong market for Filipinas because of:

> prospects of economic growth, increased labor force participation rate (especially of women), increased median of monthly domestic household income and preference of young Chinese families and expatriates for Filipino domestic helpers.[16]

By 2006, the Philippine government implemented the so-called "Super Maid" program aimed at training prospective domestic workers in CPR and other kinds of basic emergency health care.[17] Supposedly intended to help prospective migrant women to command higher wages from their employers, the program makes evident that markets for domestic workers are an important source of revenue that the Philippine state is eager to invest in.

Statistics on women's migration from the Philippines confirm that the state has been hugely successful in mobilizing women for overseas work in gendered forms of employment. According to the POEA's statistics, of the top ten job categories for newly deployed migrants, household service worker was the number one job category. An overwhelming majority (almost 96 percent) of these workers are women (Table 2). Filipina women actually dominate in different labor markets for household and related workers. For over a decade, for instance, Filipinas constituted the majority of migrant domestic workers in Hong Kong and Singapore.[18]

Table 2. Deployed Overseas Filipino Workers — New Hires, 2008,
Top Ten Skills by Sex (POEA)

Skills	Male	Female	Total
Household Service Workers	2,240	47,842	50,082
Waiters, Bartenders, and Related Workers	5,183	8,728	13,911
Charworkers, Cleaners, and Related Workers	1,851	9,769	11,620
Nurses Professional	1,556	9,939	11,495
Caregivers and Caretakers	595	9,514	10,109
Laborers/Helpers General	8,175	1,536	9,711
Plumbers and Pipe Fitters	9,643	21	9,664
Wiremen Electrical	8,812	81	8,893
Welders and Flame-Cutters	6,746	31	6,777
Caretakers Building	1,139	5,471	6,610
Other Skills	128,988	70,406	199,394
Total Deployment	174,928	163,338	338,266

Source: POEA.

Jobs understood as more "masculine," such as construction work
or even IT work, are equally prevalent throughout the world, and
the Philippine state pays attention to economic developments in different countries to identify labor markets for these types of jobs. For
instance, a labor market report posted in 2007 notes:

> Due to the economic boom in the Kingdom of Saudi Arabia, the Saudi
> government has announced mega projects in the country, such as the
> Economic Cities in Rabigh and Jizan, railway projects linking east and
> west of the Kingdom, petrochemical projects, new hospitals, new univer-
> sities and a wave of new industries. Major companies like Saudi Aramco
> and Saudi Basic Industries (SABIC) will need more engineers and con-
> struction workers until 2010 to work on $95 million worth of projects in
> the Kingdom.[19]

Similarly, another 2007 report of market prospects in Asia states:

> The region's continued economic growth has resulted to construction of
> major infrastructures and industrial projects. Consequently, it has induced
> a steady increase in the demand for foreign workers such as professionals
> (engineers, teachers, and IT workers) and skilled workers.

Recent statistics on newly deployed workers as seen in Table 2 indicate that under the category of "Plumbers and Pipe Fitters," "Laborers/Helpers (General)," and "Wiremen Electrical," all occupations likely to be engaged in infrastructure or industrial projects are filled mainly by men.

Labor market information generated through these market reports enables the Philippine state to proactively market Philippine workers to foreign employers. "Market missions" have long been successful in facilitating outflows of Philippine labor. During "marketing missions," a bureaucrat at the POEA's Marketing Branch explained, representatives from the different migration agencies "meet with governments and prospective employers and will [visit] existing employers." The purpose of marketing missions is to generate interest in Philippine workers among prospective employers as well as to initiate discussions with foreign governments on the possibilities of formalizing inflows of Philippine workers.

One high-ranking migration official in ILAS recounted his participation in early market promotions work:

> In the early 1970s, I was part of the team that organized marketing missions in the United States. There we put together the biggest construction contractors along with Philippine private labor recruiters to talk about partnerships. The reason why we went to the United States was because it was U.S. companies that had operations in the Middle East. They were the ones behind the construction boom in the Middle East. So, instead of dealing with these companies' Middle Eastern middlemen, we went straight to the head offices to get a head start over other bidders of foreign labor.

Filipinos' employment in Saudi Arabia, as this interview suggests, is linked to the globalized expansion of the U.S. construction industry. Yet the market promotions the Philippine state has done since then have perhaps been equally important to sustained Philippine out-migration to Saudi Arabia, which is among the top ten destination countries for migrants from the Philippines. As of 2007, in fact, it was the number one destination for Philippine workers.[20]

I learned during the course of my field research in 2000–2001 that the POEA was in the process of planning marketing missions to countries like Palau, Taiwan, and Israel. The 2001 POEA *Annual*

2007   Azerbaijan, Canada, Taiwan, United Arab Emirates

2006   not available

2005   Bahrain, Cyprus, Qatar, Taiwan, United Arab Emirates

2004   Korea, Kuwait, Lebanon, Taiwan, United Arab Emirates

2003   Croatia, Indonesia, Ireland, Korea, Slovenia, Taiwan,
        United Kingdom

Figure 14. Marketing missions, 2003–7. Source: POEA.

Report confirmed that in fact, marketing missions were conducted to
Taiwan (three times), the United Kingdom, the Netherlands, Nor-
way, Ireland, Israel, and Japan. According to the most recent POEA
Annual Report for 2007, missions took place to Azerbaijan, Canada,
Taiwan, and the United Arab Emirates. Figure 14 lists the POEA's
market missions since 2003. The various kinds of missions the POEA
plans and invests in demonstrate the Philippine state's global reach.
The state, moreover, is willing to pour its resources into missions in
a range of countries including politically beleaguered countries like
Israel, to "tiger" economies like Taiwan and Korea, to eastern European countries like Slovenia and Croatia, as well as to traditional
immigration countries like the United Kingdom. ˙

One official at the DFA explained that there are "times when
specific requests [for Filipino workers] are made by foreign governments." The fact that foreign states themselves make direct requests
for Philippine labor from government officials seems to suggest that
the Philippine state has been able to successfully project itself internationally as a labor brokerage state. Perhaps as a testament to the
effectiveness of the Philippine state's active marketing of Philippine
workers globally, it now plays host to delegations from overseas seeking to employ Filipino and Filipina workers. In 2001, members of
the Norwegian government came to the Philippines to "work out
manpower provisions." More recently, the POEA hosted the visits of foreign delegations from four provinces of Canada, namely,
Alberta, Saskatchewan, Manitoba, and British Columbia, as well as
from Cyprus, the United Arab Emirates, and Azerbaijan.

"Filipino Workers:
Moving the World Today"

The Philippines' migration agencies often draw on commercial marketing strategies to promote Philippine labor for export. For example, in addition to producing the glossy brochures that I discuss in the introductory section of this chapter, the staff of the POEA's Marketing Branch planned to reintroduce a so-called "direct mailer" campaign targeting the IT industries in Germany and the United States. The Marketing Branch had even created a "Hotel Promotional Linkage" program through which it distributes flyers at hotel business centers in the Philippines for business tourists. Additionally, coordinating with the Department of Trade and Investment, the Marketing Branch has organized exhibits on Filipino migrant labor at international trade fairs.

Examining the representations of Philippine workers by officials responsible for so-called market "promotions" and in the state's marketing materials demonstrates how the Philippine state circulates Filipina and Filipino bodies in the global marketplace. In the same brochure I discussed at the beginning of this chapter, the section on Filipino medical workers states that "the strong desire to heal and help people make Filipino medical workers much preferred," which echoes the remarks made by a POEA official during an interview. She commented that despite the fact that the U.K. was increasingly securing nurses from China and that the United States was securing nurses from India, "The Philippines is still top. Filipinas have a warmth and care that people like." This brochure, along with the official's comment, illustrates how the Philippine state plays a key role in producing specific sets of discourses of Filipina women. Moreover, these discourses can be traced to longer histories of Filipina nurses, as I describe in chapter 1. While many scholars have focused on the ways labor recruitment agencies or even labor-receiving countries play a role in producing and legitimating specific discursive constructions of Filipina workers, it is important to link these discourses to those long (re)produced by the Philippine state.[21]

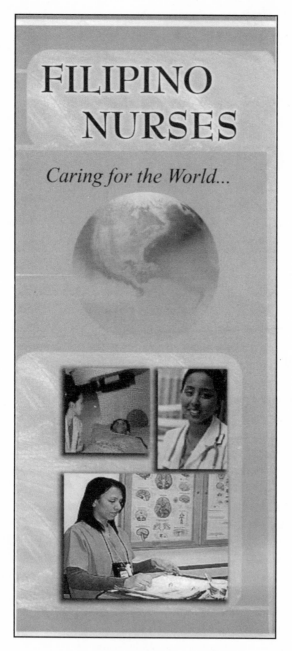

Figure 15. Brochure produced by the Philippine
Overseas Employment Administration.

A separate brochure for seafarers entitled "The Filipino Seafarer: Taking the Lead," describes to prospective employers how they are "among the most sought-after seafarers in the world today." The brochure explains this as a result of

> the dynamic development of the Filipino mariner's skill and competence over time. His affinity to the sea comes from living in an archipelago of more than 7,100 islands with a vast coastline. His history as a seafarer dates back to the 15th century when Filipino ancestors were heavily engaged in barter trading with neighboring Asian countries. During the 16th century, Filipinos manned galleons and worked hand-in-hand with Spanish seamen honing their navigational skills. And between the 18th and 19th centuries, they served as helmsmen or quartermasters aboard American ships sailing in the Pacific.

Colonialism is represented here as having helped hone the skills of Filipino seafarers. Histories of imperial violence and coerced labor are revisioned and sanitized.

To hire Filipinos, then, is to hire workers who offer distinctive cultural attitudes, embodied capacities, and skills that make them ostensibly more desirable than other nationalities of workers. Not only does the state train a wide range of workers (through the migration bureaucracy) who can perform a vast array of jobs (from construction to hotel workers, medical workers to professional/managerial), the state can guarantee employers specific kinds of racialized workers — Filipino workers — who possess essentialized traits. Moreover, these workers, inheriting specific histories of colonialism as Filipinos, namely, Spanish and American, have been left with skills that make them especially productive workers.

What the Philippine state's marketing strategies also reveal is how nationality or national difference figures in the construction of labor in a globalized labor market as specific nationals are ascribed, by their states, to have particularized skill sets or cultural sensibilities. Today's global economy functions on a global division of labor that ultimately rests on a national logic. National difference is necessary to the racialized (and gendered) work hierarchies on which the global division of labor, and hence capitalism's profits, depends. Under conditions of globalized production which also operates under conditions of international migration, different states are distinguished as possessing a kind of national labor "specialization." Different nation-states are distinguished as possessing a kind of national "specialization."

I found the workers often had a sense of pride in their distinction as Filipino workers. Roberto, for example, describes how in Taiwan the factory where he was employed hired only Filipinos, because the employers believe workers from the Philippines are " '*masipag*' [hardworking] and listen to instructions." Similarly Mike, a former seafarer, told me that "Filipino seamen are number one." "Why are we in demand?" he went on to explain, "because of English communication and we are *masipag*." Mike uses the same term as Roberto to describe what makes Filipino workers distinct.

Chiari, a dentist by profession but enrolled in a caregiver program to try to get authorization for employment in the United States, claims, "Most of us, Filipinos, as you can see, we are more patient. It's our characteristic. It's a very, very important virtue if you will take a caregiver course because we're going to take care of children . . . old persons. So you really, really have to have that much patience."[22]

Workers' identification with the putative national attributes of being "hardworking" or "patient," however unwittingly, reifies the Philippine state's construction of culturalist notions of Philippine labor. Though understandably a source of pride and dignity for people who are forced to have to work far from home, these cultural nationalist ideas can serve to reproduce racialized differences in the workplace and therefore undermine worker solidarity. At the same time, I would argue, following Brooks, that the Philippine state uses "notions of culture to pathologize working conditions," and thereby places the blame on culture for exploitation or abuse, "rather than on production imperatives."[23] Of course, nationalisms are pliable and can be reimagined in important ways. Activists in Migrante International, a transnational alliance of Philippine migrant workers, for instance, mobilize around a nationalist politics that is critical of the Philippine state's neoliberal orientation. They have also built coalitions with migrants from a broad range of ethnic and racialized

backgrounds to unite in wage and employment struggles as well as to
fight for migrants' rights around the world.

Negotiating Transfers of Migrant Workers

Though the Philippine government uses marketing techniques that
are similar to the kinds of advertising strategies used in commercial retail (that is, brochures, direct mailers, etc.), since labor is
less mobile than other kinds of commodities because it is subject
to stringent regulations (that is, visa requirements), the Philippine
state necessarily has to engage in diplomatic relations with labor-
importing countries if it aims to continue to export labor to existing
and new markets. The Philippines has a stake in initiatives taken by
labor-importing states to introduce new visa categories that allow for
the legal in-flow of migrant labor into their countries, as I have demonstrated above. However, the Philippines actively tries to initiate
bilateral labor agreements and other forms of mutual understanding
with labor-importing states to help facilitate the migration of Filipinos. Hence, to "promote" or "market" Filipino labor, officials from
the Department of Foreign Affairs (that is, embassy and consular
staff) become so important. The kinds of diplomatic relations the
Philippine state engages in range from informal networking activities
to formalized agreements.

In the Philippines, POEA officials, specifically those in the
Marketing Branch, initiate and build informal relations with the rep-
resentatives of the Philippine-based embassies of countries receiving
Philippine workers as well as prospective new "clients":

> We approach embassies. We have a "Greet a Client" program where on
> national holidays we send them flowers or other gifts and we participate
> in the activities they sponsor. This is a yearly project. We do embassy
> liaisoning with the diplomatic corps of the embassies. This is PR [public
> relations] work. We even participate in celebrations when someone is sent
> to a new post.

Maintaining existing relations and establishing new relations with
prospective "client" states includes social networking with foreign

embassies. I learned that these "liaison" activities lay the groundwork for more formal labor agreements.

If Philippines-based officials engage in informal "public relations" campaigns to market Filipino workers, the diplomatic corps does the same overseas. As staff from the Marketing Branch explained, international conferences become important venues for the promotion of Filipino workers, and marketing missions are timed to take place at the same time; side meetings are arranged with prospective employers.

International conferences are not only the place where Philippine officials promote Filipino workers; they are also the place where foreign officials make requests for Filipino workers. A top-ranking official at the Department of Foreign Affairs recounted one example of this:

> I was approached at the Beijing Review [of the U.N. Summit on Women] in New York by a woman who heads the Commission on Women in the Japanese prime minister's office. She had proposed the possibility of setting up a program for home care workers from the Philippines. With Japan's elderly population increasing and the continuing need for child care, they are looking to bring in foreign workers to fill those positions. The program would ensure that workers would get proper training and social security benefits. I thought it was a very good idea and there are now prospects of a Joint Commission Meeting on Women that will include this discussion.

By 2004 an agreement between the Philippines and Japan was formalized.[24]

Bilateral relations, mainly in the form of bilateral labor agreements (BLAs) or memorandums of understanding (MOUs), have been a key mechanism by which the Philippine government facilitates flows of Philippine labor to key overseas markets. According to one POEA official:

> Market development activities include getting into negotiations with foreign governments bilaterally and multilaterally like at international forums such as the ILO (International Labor Organization), APEC (Asia Pacific Economic Cooperation), East Asian Growth Area, the ASEAN (Association of South East Asian Nations) Labor Ministries annual meetings, IOM (International Organization for Migration), and the International

Maritime Association. The POEA provides the strategic dirty work of labor diplomacy. It is part of our strategy of diplomatic relations.

"Labor diplomacy," as Philippine migration officials describe it, is the more formalized state-to-state relations the Philippine state engages in to develop markets for Philippine labor. Different branches of the Philippine migration apparatus engage in labor diplomacy. As this official describes it, the POEA's work is to engage in the "strategic dirty work" of labor negotiations, which involves, dealings with states through a range of multilateral formations as well as engaging in more informal relations with foreign diplomatic staff in the Philippines as I described in a section above.

As of August 2000, while I was conducting field research, the Philippines had either a BLA or an MOU with a total of seventeen different countries.[25] Among the provisions contained in the BLAs or MOUs are those relating to the expansion of overseas employment and the streamlining of the bureaucratic processes necessary for workers to go abroad. For instance, one of the key provisions of the Philippines' bilateral labor agreement with Libya is "exchange of information on relevant studies and researches, technical expertise to enhance employment promotion and labor administration."[26] The exact provision is found in the bilateral agreements with the governments of Jordan and Iraq, while similar language can be found in the bilateral agreements with the governments of Kuwait, CNMI, the Federated States of Micronesia, and Qatar.[27] According to the Department of Labor and Employment, one of the four strategies guiding bilateralism is to facilitate the "more efficient mobilization process . . . [and] liberalization of entry regulations to labor-short economies." In other words, bilateralism formalizes and institutionalizes mechanisms by which labor is transferred. Not only does it formalize and institutionalize the transfer of labor; it ensures that the process is better rationalized.

The Philippines' proposed bilateral agreements with Brunei, Japan, Palau, Singapore, South Korea, Taiwan, Bahrain, Lebanon, Oman, the United Arab Emirates, Belgium, France, Greece, and the Netherlands at the time of my field research likewise center on the expansion

Country/Province	Title and Type of Bilateral Agreement/Understanding
Alberta	Memorandum of Understanding (on labor and human resources development)
Azerbaijan	Memorandum of Understanding (on labor cooperation)
British Columbia	Memorandum of Understanding (on cooperation in human resources)
Croatia	Bilateral Labor Agreement
Malaysia	Memorandum of Understanding (on migrant workers)
Manitoba	Memorandum of Understanding
Qatar	Memorandum of Understanding (on the additional protocol to labor agreements)
Singapore	Memorandum of Understanding
Taiwan	Memorandum of Understanding (on the SHPT, abolition of affidavit on fees and salaries of OFWs, review of onsite fees and charges from workers, problems on working conditions of Filipino fishermen, among others)
United Arab Emirates	Memorandum of Understanding (in the field of manpower)

Figure 16. Bilateral agreements, 2007. Source: POEA.

of overseas employment to these countries and the more rationalized and streamlined deployment of migrants, but they also contain provisions relating to the maintenance of certain standards of employment qualification. That is, they require that Filipino workers demonstrate some degree of training or skill to qualify for particular jobs.

Figure 16 summarizes data from the POEA's 2007 *Annual Report,* noting the countries the Philippines has attempted to negotiate more formal diplomatic relations with on the issue of labor migration.[28]

Bilateral labor agreements, however, require that the Philippine state strike a balance between its interests in expanding markets for Filipino and Filipina labor and its interests in maintaining other economic or geopolitical relations with foreign states. According to another POEA bureaucrat,

> Bilateral agreements are formed with an understanding of the general foreign policy context outlined by Joint Commission Meetings (JCMs) and/or Memorandums of Understanding (MOUs) between the Philippines and specific countries. The JCM or the MOU are a kind of "umbrella" providing the context for labor agreements. We at the POEA handle these agreements, but we have to work with the regional desks of the Department of Foreign Affairs who handle JCMs and MOUs.

Philippine migration agencies, as this quotation indicates, can make bilateral labor agreements with particular states only if they have a broader understanding of the Philippines' diplomatic relations with those countries. One official at the DFA explained:

> Each agreement must be analyzed within the context of overall relations between the Philippines and that country as well as overall relations in the region, including multilateral relations in ASEAN or other groupings. For example if the Philippines signs an agreement with Myanmar, it may have implications for the Philippines' relations with other ASEAN states. Timing is key as is the overall climate of political and economic relations.

An ILAS official provided another example of how different sets of diplomatic relations impact the Philippines' ability to negotiate bilaterally around labor migration with specific states:

> Our challenges with labor diplomacy are reflected, for example, in Taiwan because of the one-China policy. The Philippines has a pseudo "embassy" in Taiwan which is officially not an embassy but is de facto an embassy. It acts as a private corporation but it performs governmental functions. The dealings with the Taiwanese become difficult because you can't go as public officials. Government officials go as private citizens who go on speaking engagements in Taiwan, for instance, while setting up meetings on the side with local officials.

Though the Philippines sends workers to both China and Taiwan, as this quotation makes clear, it must also make sure not to threaten overall diplomatic relations with both countries, since the Philippines officially has a one-China policy.

While the Philippine state competes with other labor-exporting states for a share of the global labor market, it also attempts to cooperate with certain labor-exporting states in ways that can be mutually beneficial to all parties.

> The Philippines is attempting to create a niche in skilled labor while Vietnam provides more unskilled labor, but there is a drive toward regional complementation among labor-sending countries. For example, there is a proposed complementation in market promotions with Vietnam, which packages both Philippine and Vietnamese labor to prospective employers where the Philippines offers to provide potential employers with skilled and managerial staff while Vietnam pledges to provide unskilled labor.

"Regional complementation" is an example of the innovative forms of labor diplomacy the Philippine state engages in to distribute migrant workers globally. Of course, professionals generate more money for the Philippines. In 2007, for example, the POEA announced that "the increasing number of deployed professional and skilled workers caused the steady increase of remittances by overseas Filipino workers."[29]

The Philippine government's role in marketing Filipino workers and engaging in diplomatic relations with foreign governments is both for the purpose of promoting the deployment of migrants through Philippine-based private recruitment agencies as well as through its own government recruitment facility, the Government Placement Branch (GPB). In a marketing mission in 1998 to the United Kingdom, for instance, the Philippines explored the possibilities of deploying Filipino nurses to meet the demand for what was estimated as fifteen thousand vacancies. Furthermore, the POEA met with U.K. hiring agencies, demonstrating a willingness to recruit workers directly through the POEA's GPB.

The GPB supports the private labor recruitment industry. A Marketing Branch official states, "During marketing missions, the Marketing Branch doesn't distinguish between the GPB and private recruiters. It markets for the whole industry." However, the GPB to some extent competes with private recruitment agencies, a fact acknowledged by POEA officials: "The Government Placement Branch is important, but the private sector doesn't like it. The GPB isn't about 'hard sell.' It captures those markets that don't want to go through private recruiters."

The GPB is the agency that foreign states deal with to secure migrant labor for government-to-government hiring. Rather than allowing private recruitment agencies access to potentially huge foreign government clients, the Philippine state positions itself as the provider of labor for these government labor contracts. "When there are foreign diplomatic dealings and foreign labor officials request labor of the President, the GPB steps in. We can't recommend private recruiters." The state sees itself as being a more ideal provider of migrant labor to foreign governments than private recruitment agencies because the transfers of labor between governments become a diplomatic matter. Furthermore, the state ensures that workers are properly trained and certified and conveniently spares foreign governments the effort of trying to locate appropriate recruitment agencies.

The POEA official responsible for the GPB described the various client states it has and the kinds of labor it supplies to them:

> Our governmental clients include the Ministries of Health, for example, of the Kingdom of Saudi Arabia, specifically bigger government hospitals. The governments of Fiji and Libya are also our clients; we provide workers to their state hospitals as well, but we're having some problems with them. There are also some private employers that get workers through the GPB from these countries. The government of Qatar is also a client for medical personnel. The Ministry of Education in Papua New Guinea is a client. We supply workers for the Water Systems and Royal Navy of Abu Dhabi. The GPB also recruits for Saudi Airlines and Catering as well as Royal Brunei Airways and Catering. Private clients are usually those who do not want to deal with private agencies. They are for very specific and technical jobs. In Saipan, for example, we have a publishing house as a client. The GPB has a special relationship with Taiwan. A Memorandum of Agreement signed between the Philippines and Taiwan allows for specific private employers to deal exclusively with the Philippine government. These include Acer and Nanyang, they are electronics companies, which hire both general and skilled workers.

The GPB had twenty foreign government clients at the time of my field research in 2000–2001. The biggest demand from these clients, as this quotation indicates, is for medical personnel in government hospitals. Additionally, the GPB has some private-sector clients. In addition to the ones mentioned by this official, the GPB provides physical therapists to the United States and IT workers to Singapore. As of 2007, the GPB had seventeen government clients.

The fact that the GPB has a number of government clients suggests that with increasing privatization states are "outsourcing" government workers, securing migrants from other countries rather than its own citizens and nationals.

The term "labor brokerage" suggests not only that the state distributes labor globally, but must do so through a process of negotiations, most critically with labor-importing states. Yet for a developing state like the Philippines, successfully securing bilateral labor agreements or other kinds of formal understandings regarding migrant labor requires that the state curtail the distribution of Filipino workers when necessary.

In the Asian crisis, for instance, the question of how different labor-importing countries would address the issue of migrant workers became particularly urgent as states throughout the region had to deal with the consequences of massive economic dislocation. South Korea, which experienced some of the most severe forms of dislocation leading to the IMF crisis, introduced a repatriation policy, the only country in the region to do so.[30] The Philippines, according to one researcher, was best equipped among the various sending countries to deal with the potential influx of returning workers. He argues, "The Philippine Congress had the foresight to provide for the establishment of administrative machinery for the purpose of dealing with return migration under the Migrant Workers and Overseas Filipinos Act of 1995." However, I believe Lund and Panda's formulation is more apt. They describe the expulsion of migrant workers in the wake of the Asian crisis as "involuntary return migration or mobility."[31] In the case of Philippine migrants, the Philippine state performs a role in the forced return migration of workers.

Even in the absence of severe economic crisis, as in the case of the Asian crisis, migrants can be a source of political problems for labor-importing states if local workers see foreign workers as unfairly competing for jobs. The perceived excess of foreign labor by native workers in host countries can be politically contentious. Philippine marketing efforts are attuned to the potential controversy that accompanies the entrance of foreign workers into particular countries. As I described in chapter 2, the Philippines'

migration agencies responsible for labor market information genera-
tion therefore attempt to identify job openings and accompanying
visa categories in different countries while also being careful to
alert prospective migrants about the closure of markets or new visa
restrictions in order to regulate their outflows.

The Philippine state coordinates with host countries in attempting to manage undocumented migration. When Israel, in 2003, issued
plans to crack down on undocumented migrants, Philippine migration officials made sure to advise Filipinos to enter the country legally.
According to a public statement issued by the Philippine embassy
in Israel, "Those who wish to work in Israel must be properly documented, or they will risk being arrested and immediately deported."[32]
Meanwhile, the Philippine embassy in Israel requested the Israeli government to abate the mass deportation of migrants, cooperating with
Israel to ensure that undocumented migrants availed themselves of
mechanisms to legalize their status.[33]

If economic crisis and the contraction of jobs in labor-importing
states necessitate the repatriation of workers, or political crisis and
concerns about undocumented migrants require the deportation of
migrants, the crisis of war has opposite effects. According to an ILAS
official:

> During the Gulf War, the Saudi leadership appealed to the Philippines to
> encourage people to stay rather than evacuate. The fear on the part of
> the Saudi Arabians was that without Filipinos, their economy would fall.
> As a result, the Philippines had to show workers that it was safe to stay
> in Saudi Arabia, going around, for instance, without gas masks to show
> workers that they had nothing to fear.

The Philippine state has well-developed transnational apparatuses
that not only export labor; it also has the capacity to repatriate workers should they pose problems to host states. This is an important
mechanism by which the Philippine state is able to reproduce its system of labor export: it is able to ensure foreign states and employers
not only that they will be able to take advantage of cheap foreign
labor, but that the Philippine state will intervene when its citizens are
redundant or even politically problematic. While the Philippine state
has an interest in guaranteeing outflows of labor through bilateral

agreements, this must be balanced against the interests of labor-importing states. Labor-receiving states may demand cheaper migrant labor, but they must also contend with demands for employment by their nationals in the case of domestic economic crises. Furthermore, if labor-importing states face the crisis of war, as in the case of Saudi Arabia, the Philippine state even uses its migration apparatus to compel workers to stay in their places of employment if it suits their employers.

Conclusion

Through an examination of the mechanisms by which the Philippine state exports migrants globally, we come to see how a "peripheral" state plays a critical role in the globalization of labor. Global production is giving rise to a reorganization of work and demands for gendered and racialized flexible labor. The labor brokerage state, meanwhile, exploits this labor demand for its own purposes. By examining the processes by which the Philippine state distributes labor around the world, it becomes clear that international labor mobility is a product of globalized trade in labor that depends on relations and negotiations between states. The Philippine state does not operate in isolation when it brokers Filipino labor.

While the Philippine state has an interest in guaranteeing outflows of labor through bilateral agreements, it balances these interests against the interests of labor-importing states. These states may demand cheaper migrant labor, but they must also contend with their nationals' demands for employment. Migrants can be a source of problems for labor-importing states if local workers believe foreigners unfairly take away their jobs. Accordingly, the Philippine state has developed mechanisms by which it not only exports labor but by which it forcibly repatriates workers. As I will show in chapter 6, the Philippine state even uses these mechanisms to discipline workers for foreign employers.

4

New National Heroes
Patriotism and Citizenship Reconfigured

The week of the signing of the Migrant Workers and Overseas Filipinos Act of 1995, or Republic Act 8042 (RA8042), was officially
declared "Migrant Heroes Week" by the Philippine government. All
the Philippines' migration agencies mark the signing of RA8042 with
commemorative activities every June to showcase the expanded support and assistance Philippine government agencies in the Philippines
and throughout the world promise to Philippine citizens working
abroad.

The opening ceremonies for Migrant Heroes Week in 2000,
however, seemed especially significant for migration officials at the
POEA, given that 2000 was declared "The Year of the Overseas Filipino Worker" by then–Philippine president Joseph Estrada. The main
entrance of the POEA was flanked by a huge mural depicting a man
and a woman standing atop the globe with hands clasped and arms
raised triumphantly. Nearly all of the several hundred chairs in the
main foyer as well as the additional chairs set up for the occasion
were filled before the event's official start. Additionally, the back
wall of the foyer was lined with people while others were queued just
outside. In all, there were more than five hundred people present
by the time the opening activities of Migrant Heroes Week 2000
commenced. Most of the people present were prospective migrants
waiting to have their documents processed at the POEA.

The motto "Migranteng Pinoy Kabalikat sa Pag-Angat sa 2000"
(Migrant Filipinos Side by Side for Progress in 2000) was emblazoned on banners, balloons, and the sashes adorning flower bouquets

scattered throughout the foyer. The program featured an assortment of high-ranking government officials "including the undersecretary of the Department of Foreign Affairs and the Philippine Overseas Employment Administration's administrator" as well as a representative from President Joseph Estrada's office. All of the officials who spoke repeatedly thanked and praised migrant workers for their economic contributions to the Philippine economy, often characterizing them as "heroic."

The program was interrupted, however, by the clamor of protesters from the Philippine-based groups of the transnational alliance of grassroots Philippine migrant organizations, Migrante International, gathered just outside the POEA compound. "It's time people wake up to the wrongdoing of the government. Where is the protection of workers?" an activist on a megaphone demanded

Not to be deterred, the undersecretary of the Department of Labor and Employment (DOLE) began his speech with his own rallying cry, raising his fist and calling out, "Mabuhay ang POEA!" (Long live the POEA!) "Mabuhay ang OWWA!" (Long live the Overseas Workers Welfare Administration!) "Mabuhay ang DOLE!" (Long live the DOLE!)" Many in the audience joined him. He proceeded to relay an account of the experience in a Riyadh jail of the Philippine ambassador to Saudi Arabia. The ambassador, according to the undersecretary, was trying to negotiate the release of detained Philippine migrants:

> The ambassador asked, "Who is Filipino?" Everyone in the jail raised their hands. The funny thing is that Bangladeshis and migrants from other places raised their hands along with the Filipinos. The moral of the story is that everybody wants to be Filipino because they know that the Philippine government helps its workers.

Against the persistent shouts of activists, the undersecretary claimed that "without overseas labor the Philippines could have had a social revolution. With so many entering the labor force, where could they go? Overseas work became an economic and political solution for our country." Many in the audience applauded approvingly. He went on to state:

VISION: To be a culturally-sensitive, customer-driven and business-oriented advocate of the Overseas Filipino Workers' well-being.

MISSION: To ensure quality employment for Overseas Filipino Workers

Figure 17. Brochure produced by the Philippine Overseas Employment Administration. The motto "Angat Pinoy 2004" is at the bottom left.

> Philippine territory goes beyond what we once knew. It extends now to
> Australia, to the United States, and etc. What used to be Bayang Filipino
> [Filipino Nation] is now Mundong Filipino [Filipino World].

Ignoring the commotion outside, the recipient of 2000's "Migrant
Hero of the Year" award, a male migrant worker, echoed the POEA's
motto on the "partnership" role migrants should assume in relation
to the Philippine state. Closing the day's program, he stated:

> OFWs [overseas Filipino workers] are ambassadors of goodwill. We do
> it gladly out of loyalty to the Philippines. With all the political strife
> in the country, we OFWs want to work with the government and the
> private sector. Training and development [of OFWs] is necessary to live
> up to international standards, to open more jobs, and hence to help the
> Philippines.

Through rituals like the celebrations of Migrant Heroes Week or the
Year of the Overseas Filipino Worker the state represents idealized
notions of state–citizen relations and Philippine nationalism within
the context of international migration, even as these representations
are fiercely contested by the migrants themselves. As I discuss in the
chapter that follows, migrants have demanded that the Philippine
state offer more protections to the "heroes" it profits from. Still, the
Philippine state is invested in (re)producing specific kinds of relations
with its overseas workers because labor brokerage depends on it. It is
perhaps because the state faces widespread criticism of its migration
policies that it puts a tremendous effort into idealizing state–citizen
relations. It puts forward the "Migrant Hero of the Year" award recipient, for instance, as a model. Conveniently enough he represents
himself as a partner with the state in steering the country toward a
more modern future.

The Philippine state attempts to shape the migrants' sense of
membership *before* they even leave. The state is not so much trying
to "reincorporate" its erstwhile citizens as it is trying to reconfigure the very meaning of Philippine citizenship. For labor brokerage
to remain an economically profitable and politically viable developmental strategy for the Philippine state, it requires that Philippine
citizens be willing to work outside the country in faraway destinations
while at the same time maintaining their links (economic, political,

and affective) to the homeland. The Philippine state has therefore worked to actively reconfigure notions of Philippine nationalism (as "heroic" or even, "worldly") as evidenced in state practices like the celebrations of Migrant Heroes Week.[1] What has emerged can be described as *migrant citizenship* in the sense that membership in the Philippines is increasingly construed as actually requiring employment overseas. The discourse on "rights" as well as responsibilities has been important for the Philippine state in constructing migrant citizenship as evidenced in the undersecretary's anecdote on the Philippine embassy's work in Saudi Arabia. The promise of "rights" in particular is a strategy by which the state tries to normalize emigration. It is a means by which the state attempts to reassure would-be migrants that though they may face uncertain futures in unfamiliar places they can enjoy the entitlements of an expanded Philippine citizenship encoded in laws like RA8042. While the state represents migrants as "heroes," it also represents itself as grateful for the labors of its migrants and committed to extending them the benefits and protections they deserve as citizens.

The state–citizen relation on which the Philippines' labor brokerage system depends is not necessarily a natural one and is often tenuous. It is, as perhaps national projects are, "imagined." The state, therefore, constantly needs to work at maintaining positive relations with its migrant citizens. Or, at the very least, the state needs to maintain a veneer of competency and dependability. After all, citizenship is made meaningful by citizen-subjects' identification in whole or in part with the nation-state. Though the very structure of migrant labor systems is such that migrants, especially if they have responsibilities or other close ties to family members or other kin in other homelands, are bound to return, the Philippine state needs to infuse migrants' linkages to the homeland with particular kinds of meaning. As Weekley argues, neoliberal states like the Philippines "must rely on appeals to the imaginary nation to meet their globalizing economic objectives. Precisely as the processes of globalization create new and deeper alienations within national societies and undermine states' power to manage them, those states must attempt to strengthen the 'social glue' that is national identity"[2]

Though scholars of international migration have focused on the ways immigration is transforming citizenship in labor-receiving countries,[3] my argument here is that migration is, just as importantly, transforming citizenship in labor-sending countries, especially as they become engaged in the brokerage of labor. As Fitzgerald argues in his study of emigration and emigrant politics and policies in Mexico, "Emigrants are in another state's grip, so governments of countries of emigration must develop creative ways to manage citizens abroad, preserve their national loyalty, and extract their resources. Their tools are primarily symbolic, though the consequences are real."[4]

In this chapter I will focus on the multiple shifting and overlapping ways the Philippine state has come to construct and reconstruct the meanings of Philippine citizenship. I pay particular attention to the kinds of nationalist duties the state attaches to national belonging as it pertains to migrants. I discuss the legal and institutional mechanisms through which citizenship as a set of responsibilities is defined while also weaving in ethnographic illustrations of the state's cultural production of ideas of nationalism, national belonging, and citizenship in rituals like Migrant Heroes Week as well as more mundane bureaucratic practices. I will turn my attention to an examination of the entitlements the Philippine state putatively extends to its overseas citizens and will explore their limits in later chapters.

Stretching the Boundaries of National Belonging and Nationalist Duty

Balikbayan

Even before the introduction of the Philippines' labor export policy in 1974 the Philippine state had already begun to introduce new ideas of nationalism both to normalize out-migration as well as to normalize migrants' sustained linkages to the Philippines in the form of remittances. For instance, as it was encouraging nurse out-migration through the EVP program in the late 1960s into the early 1970s, as I discussed in chapter 1, the Philippine government introduced the so-called *Balikbayan* (nation returnee) program in 1973. The program encouraged emigrants (mainly those in the United States) to come back "home" to the Philippines as tourists and, ultimately, as investors. So-called *balikbayans* were given special incentives, including the ability to bring in two duty- and tax-free *balikbayan* boxes in lieu of luggage upon returning to the Philippines, the opportunity to purchase up to $1000 worth of duty-free merchandise upon arrival, and even the chance to purchase land.[5] While the *Balikbayan* program was directly targeted at those who had already left the Philippines permanently, it also indirectly targeted prospective migrants. By introducing a special status to those who left the Philippines to live and work elsewhere, the state shifted public discourses around migration. Migration was often characterized at best as a "brain drain" or at worst as a form of national disloyalty.[6] Though the Philippine government under Marcos's dictatorship created the status of *balikbayan* to reincorporate its erstwhile citizens as members of the Philippine nation, it suppressed the rights of citizens living in the Philippines.

Even as it celebrated *balikbayans* and encouraged their economic contributions to the Philippines without necessarily coercing them, the Marcos administration also introduced policies that actually required those specifically working as temporary contractual workers abroad to remit their overseas earnings back to the Philippines:

> it shall be mandatory for all Filipino workers abroad to remit a portion of their foreign exchange earnings to their families, dependents and/or beneficiaries in the country in accordance with the rules and regulations prescribed by the Secretary of Labor. (Government of the Republic of the Philippines 1974)

By 1983, with Executive Order 857 Marcos further required that remittances be sent through the Philippine banking systems. Different groups of workers were required to remit different percentages of their salaries:

1. Seamen or mariners: 70 percent of basic salary

2. Workers of Filipino contractors and construction companies: 70 percent of basic salary

Figure 18. Filipino pride at Ninoy Aquino International Airport, 2008. Photograph by Ben Razon. Source: Sugar Mountain Media.

3. Doctors, engineers, teachers, nurses, and other professional workers whose contracts provide for free board and lodging: 70 percent of basic salary

4. All other professional workers whose employment contracts do not provide for free board and lodging facilities: 50 percent of basic salary

5. Domestic and other service workers: 50 percent of basic salary

6. All other workers not falling under the aforementioned categories: 50 percent of basic salary.

Migrants were mandated to sign an agreement pledging their compliance with these aspects of EO 857. Indeed, EO 857 even included punitive measures: "Contract workers who fail to comply with the requirements of this Order shall be suspended or excluded from the list of eligible workers for overseas employment. In cases of subsequent violations, he shall be repatriated from the job site at the expense of the employer or at his expense, as the case may be."

Figure 19. Currency exchange counter at the Mall of Asia, Manila, 2008. Most malls in Manila offer currency exchange services. Photograph by Ben Razon. Source: Sugar Mountain Media.

Marcos was eventually pressured to dispense with EO 857. Marcos rescinded the mandatory remittance policy not only in response to migrants' protests, but widespread protests of his dictatorship.

The Marcos administration's valorization of the *balikbayan* on the one hand and its policies demanding migrants' remittances on the other, while seemingly contradictory, partly reflect the nature of the dictatorship. The Marcoses engaged in ostentatious displays for the outside world like Muhammad Ali's "Thrilla in Manila" and the Miss Universe pageant in order to secure legitimacy on an international stage, even as they brutally lorded over Philippine citizens at home. At the same time, the administration's construction of new ideas of national belonging and its introduction of policies to regulate migrants' remittances indicate increasing the state's investment in the export of workers.

Bagong Bayani *(New Heroes)*

Marcos's successors continued to try to regulate migrants' remittances, albeit in less punitive ways. Corazon Aquino was faced with the challenge of having to retain Marcos's labor export program while simultaneously needing to distinguish her version of the program from her predecessor's. As one high-ranking Philippine official explained:

> It was with Marcos that migration was promoted for economic and political reasons. But with Aquino and the emergence of democratic institutions, the emphasis shifted away from labor export to instead a perspective that the freedom of movement should not be curtailed.

To "democratize" the Philippine international migration the state invoked new nationalist discourses. Early in her administration Aquino began to refer to Filipino migrant workers as *bagong bayani* or "new heroes."[7] By characterizing out-migration as "heroic" Aquino portrayed international migration as a voluntary act of self-sacrificing individuals living in a democratic society rather than a kind of forced conscription under a dictatorial regime. Overseas employment is represented as a sacrifice akin to those made by anticolonial nationalists: a sacrifice that requires some degree of suffering but ultimately advances the greater national good. In 1988, just a few years after ascending to power, President Aquino formally proclaimed December as the "Month of Overseas Filipinos" and even now, twenty years later, the discourse of "heroism" dominates state representations of migrant workers.

The nationalist discourse of "heroism" would also appear in migration policies related to migrants' remittances during Aquino's presidency. The POEA, for example, appended a "Code of Discipline" to migrants' employment contracts spelling out migrants' specific duties to the country, "to uphold the ideals of the Republic of the Philippines and to defend it, if warranted; to abide by the rules and regulations aimed at promoting the worker's interest and enhancing national gain."[8] The "Code of Discipline" replaced Marcos's mandatory remittance policy with a statement on nationalist duty. Migration is cast as truly "heroic" only if migrants support national developmental goals through their regular remittance sending.

As I illustrate in the vignette that opens this chapter, the state actively engages in producing and reproducing discourses of nationalism, particularly the "heroism" discourse, in highly public ways. Migrant Heroes Week, for instance, was celebrated with as much fanfare in 2001, the second year of my field research, as it was in 2000. In 2001, as in the previous year, high-ranking government officials addressed migrant workers in a series of activities at the POEA and other migration agencies where they repeated their "heroism" refrain. The undersecretary of the Department of Labor and Employment, for instance, stated,

> Best wishes to all OFWs. You have a great theme because you truly are the true heroes. I'm happy and proud we've set aside one week for honoring of migrant workers.... Our migrants have become our modern-day heroes, in our bleakest days of our economy, our bright lights.

Filomeno Aguilar finds that migrants themselves often characterize their decision to leave the Philippines as a kind of secularized religious rite of passage. He argues that "overseas employment is valued as a form of secular pilgrimage in a quest for economic bounty and life experience."[9] In the Philippine context discourses of nationalism like heroism must be understood as a secular form of religious duty. Nationalist anticolonial struggles, as Reynaldo Ileto illustrates, have often been infused with religious understandings.[10] Overseas employment becomes a sacrifice akin to those made by anticolonial nationalists: a sacrifice that requires some degree of suffering but ultimately advances the greater national good.

If the punitive measures defined by Marcos's EO 857 are no longer valid and nationalism has been deployed to encourage migrants' remittances and investments, contemporary migration policies do provide other kinds of mechanisms by which migrants can be sanctioned. Today, migrants' employment contracts contain language requiring POEA-certified migrants to remit their earnings to the Philippines: "The employer shall assist the employee in remitting a percentage of his salary through the proper banking channel."[11] "The seafarer is required to make an allotment which shall be payable once a month to his designated allottee in the Philippines through any authorized Philippine bank. The master/employer/agency shall provide the seafarer with facilities to do so at no expense to the seafarer. The allotment shall be at least eighty percent (80 percent) of the seafarer's monthly basic salary including back wages, if any."[12]

Whereas EO 857 made remittance requirements a responsibility of migrants themselves, under the new regime, employers play a role in "assisting" migrants with their remittances. Moreover, the "Code of Discipline" states, "It shall also be [migrants'] obligation to abide with the requirements on remittance earnings as well as to provide material help to his family during the period of his overseas employment." The family, therefore, becomes the site for the regulation of migrants' remittances.

Family members of migrants can enlist the POEA's Welfare Services Branch to demand that migrants send remittances regularly if they have been errant. The Welfare Services Branch sends letters to migrants on behalf of their family members that remind them of their familial duties:

> We would like to remind you that as an overseas Filipino worker it is one of your obligations to provide ample financial and moral support to your family. Make your loved ones feel your presence as though you were with them through constant communications. Failure to comply with this responsibility affects not only the socio-economic, but also the moral and mental well-being of helpless dependents, thus adversely affecting their struggle for survival. We therefore hope you understand our writing you. (Welfare Services Branch)[13]

After several warnings, workers can then be "watchlisted" and prevented from applying for future overseas work. These punitive measures are not very different from those applied under the Marcos administration. What is different, however, is that migrants' families are used as the justification for punitive measures applied by the Philippine government.

The family is an especially important institution for the Philippine state as it is the family that ensures that migrants send their remittances to the Philippines on a regular basis. As one POEA official explained, one task of his office is to try "to track down workers and bridge communications between workers and families especially when they don't send money." According to this official, the POEA's educational programs attempt to place an emphasis on "values" because government officials are concerned that workers do not send money to the Philippines or do not try to take care of family problems at home.

Familial responsibility is often represented as an extension of nationalist responsibility. For instance, a priest who opened up the ceremonies for Migrant Heroes Week of 2001 stated that migrants work overseas, "not only for their families, but for their nation. As the new heroes, may you equip your families with the values they need, may they remember the fact that you are contributing to the economy." These discourses rest on heteronormative logics that "normalize and naturalize heterosexuality and heterosexual practices including marriage, family, and biological reproduction."[14] Indeed, the children of migrants are often represented by the church as prone to homosexuality because they lack adequate parental guidance. The church employs the threat of sexual deviance among their children to sustain migrants' emotional linkages with their families, which the state hopes will sustain migrants' remittances as well.

The construction of new discourses of nationalism and the crafting of migrant citizenship must be understood within the state's broader project of reshaping Philippine national identity in ways that complement the overall restructuring of the Philippine economy around neoliberal logics. Weekley argues, for instance, that President Fidel Ramos, "openly and vigorously pursued a neoliberal economic agenda, which was intended to integrate the Philippines into the global economy." One mechanism by which Ramos attempted "to harness the political and social consent for the disruptive restructuring necessary to this agenda" was "to revive national spirit in the country."[15] In particular, the centennial activities in 1998 commemorating the Philippines' anticolonial struggle against the Spanish became a means by which the Philippine state attempted to reinterpret critical elements of Philippine history to legitimate its neoliberal program. "Freedom is the Wealth of the Nation" was the official theme for the centennial activities. However, "freedom" is construed in neoliberal terms, that is, "freedom" from state intervention (privatization and deregulation) and "freedom" in terms of trade relations (liberalization). Privatization, deregulation, and liberalization were the core elements of Ramos's so-called "Philippines 2000," a program meant to fast-track neoliberal restructuring in the Philippines. Rob Wilson comments on the role of the Asia Pacific Economic Cooperation organization (APEC), a regional grouping that promotes neoliberal orthodoxy and includes the Philippines as a central participant. He says that the work that states perform to imagine the nation is "an act of semi-joyous signifying that both props up ('structures') and distorts ('masks') the materials of social reality and works (through the production of some symbolic 'excess' to cover up the holes) to conceal and reveal (via sublimation, displacement and other defences) those social traumas and antagonisms haunting its very creation."[16] This observation aptly describes the kinds of work the Philippine state performs through the discourse of "new national heroism" as well.

Overseas Filipino Investors

Nationalism has been deployed in yet other ways by the Philippine state not only to encourage migrants' remittance sending but also to channel their remittances more directly into the state's developmental agenda. For instance, in the 1970s and 1980s, migrant workers were identified in routine government documents and bureaucratic parlance as "OCWs," or overseas contract workers. Later, after major migration policy reforms were introduced in 1995 "OCW" was replaced with "OFW," or overseas Filipino workers, emphasizing workers' nationality or citizenship as Filipinos as opposed to the nature of their work. Not long after Gloria Macapagal-Arroyo took office after President Joseph Estrada's impeachment, she introduced the term "OFI," or Overseas Filipino Investors in her state of the nation address in which she encouraged migrants to invest their overseas earnings on developmental projects in their communities or in entrepreneurial ventures.

Even before Arroyo took office, in fact, the Philippine state had introduced programs to try to get migrants to invest their remittance earnings in state-sponsored development programs. For instance, through the Commission on Filipinos Overseas (CFO), the state instituted the Lingkod sa Kapwa Pilipino or LINKAPIL program, which "provides a mechanism for the transfer of assistance from overseas Filipinos to beneficiaries in the Philippines."[17] Through LINKAPIL, migrant workers can contribute toward livelihood projects, educational initiatives, health and welfare activities, infrastructure building as well as disaster relief. According to the CFO, 869.12 million Philippine pesos was generated through the program between 1990 and 1999, benefiting projects in eighty-five provinces and cities.[18]

The CFO was also a major actor in organizing a conference of the International Network of Filipinos Overseas (INFO) in 2000. The conference was an attempt by the state to mobilize migrants as "partners in development" upon their return. According to the conference invitation letter the president (Joseph Estrada at the time) recognized "the economic and humanitarian assistance by the Overseas Filipinos to the homeland" and it encouraged attendees to "support all the programs that INFO will be presenting during the conference." Among the programs highlighted at the conference were development projects, including those sponsored by the CFO.

Just as with the "Migrant Workers' Week" events at the POEA, top-ranking officials were present at this conference, and it was an event geared toward Filipinos living and working overseas. The president was supposed to have been the keynote speaker, but faced with an impeachment trial in the Philippine Senate, he was unable to attend. The message that all of these dignitaries shared is the same message repeated time and again in multiple forms and in multiple places: that migrants are "heroes" who make contributions to their homeland through their economic contributions and that workers as "heroes" become representatives of their nation around the world. Held at the opulent Manila Hotel, the conference included several hundred Filipino migrants among the participants as well as co-organizers. In the president's speech, read by one of his cabinet members, he stressed that "the challenge of being a true Filipino is to be able to transcend boundaries and politics. We'll be judged by what we've done for our motherland and our fellow countrymen."

Migrants, as authentic Filipinos, this statement suggests, are to contribute to the Philippines by not allowing national boundaries, or even political differences, perhaps with the government, to get in the way.

What migrants can do as citizens is to continue to work overseas, as another government official suggests: "Our best hope, during the [economic and political] crisis is export in the information technology industry. Forget about the 'brain drain.' As much as we can, we need to beat the Indians, the Taiwanese, etc. Anyways, we could replace who leaves [overseas jobs]." Here we see that the state attempts to link Filipino migrants' overseas employment with national development. Filipinos must work overseas and surpass the overseas workers of other labor-sending states, replacing them, in this case in information technology jobs. Filipino migrants offer hope to the Philippine economy by diligently working overseas.

Celebrating Returns

If the Philippine state encourages migrants to maintain their links to the homeland as investors, it also affirms migrants' return home between contracts. The state needs migrants' remittances as well as their return to the Philippines in between employment contracts to continue to benefit from and to reproduce the labor brokerage regime. Migrants are expected to abide by the terms of their temporary employment contracts and to return to the Philippines at the conclusion of a contract before embarking on another contract overseas, rather than staying in their countries of employment and therefore violating immigration laws in their host countries. For the Philippines' labor brokerage regime to continue to maintain its global standing as a reliable reserve of temporary, "flexible" workers, migrants' compliance with the terms of their employment contracts and work visas by returning to the Philippines is critically important.

Migrants' return has become a highly celebrated event. During the month of December, when most migrants come back to the Philippines for brief holiday breaks with their families, the Philippine state celebrates a festive "heroes' welcome" at the Ninoy Aquino International Airport in Manila. Former President Fidel Ramos, Estrada's predecessor, initiated this practice in 1993, which became a yearly event like the celebration of Migrant Heroes Week in June.

The heroes' welcome activities of 2000 took place at the height of President Joseph Estrada's controversial impeachment trial. Fast losing support in the Philippines, Estrada attempted to appeal to returning migrants for support through the annual heroes' welcome activities at the airport. Accompanied by dignitaries, including the secretary of the Department of Tourism, the secretary of the DOLE, the administrators of the POEA and the OWWA, the secretary of the Bureau of Immigration, and other officials, the president greeted migrants returning from Saudi Arabia, the first major flight of migrant workers to arrive for the holiday season. As the migrants approached the presidential entourage, they were given white caps reading "OFW-2000 'Bayan' mo, bilib sa 'yo'" (OFW-2000 "Your country believes in you"), the theme for 2000's heroes' welcome festivities. Along the main highway leading from the airport to the main arteries of Metro Manila, street lamps were decorated with signs reading the same slogan. Selected workers won cash prizes, free plane tickets, a catered meal in the airport's VIP lounge, and a chance to socialize with the dignitaries.

Many of the workers stopped to put down their heavy bags of *pasalubong* (souvenir gifts) and their carry-on luggage to rush up and greet the president, excitedly shaking his hand. Even I found myself caught up in the excitement of possibly meeting the president. It is not often that one is able to actually meet a head of state. The significance of workers' being able to meet the president of their country cannot be overestimated. Many of those deplaning the flight from Saudi Arabia were likely employed as domestic helpers or construction and service workers and therefore occupying positions in society far removed from the seats of political power. Given the crisis the president was faced with at the time, this particular public appearance was crucial for him. Migrant workers had been visibly part of the debate about whether the president should be impeached — calling in to various radio and television news programs to voice their

opinions, writing to newspapers, and in some cases organizing themselves overseas to either support or denounce the president. While
the heroes' welcome is typically aimed at honoring migrants for their
heroic sacrifice of working abroad and, perhaps more importantly, to
praise them for coming back home, this particular heroes' welcome
also became an opportunity for the president to curry favor with
returning citizens during a moment of political crisis.

Conclusion

This chapter has illustrated how the Philippine state has reconfigured citizenship for migrant workers as a means of both facilitating
their out-migration while encouraging their sustained linkages to the
homeland. Citizenship, however, is also defined as sets of obligations with remittance sending perhaps one of the most important
duties of an overseas Philippine citizen. Remittances are secured
through nationalist discourses, but they are also secured through discourses around familial responsibility. Some of the same institutions
that are supposedly meant to provide protections become means of
disciplining, regulating, and controlling citizens' obligations.

Migrant Heroes celebrations and other similar activities take place
in the Philippines at the government's migration offices, not abroad.
They are aimed not at emigrants, but at prospective migrants and
migrant returnees. Scholars of international migration have focused
on the ways labor-sending states attempt to reincorporate their erstwhile citizens extraterritorially as a means of sustaining migrants'
remittances though they may be settled abroad. My point here is
to illustrate the kinds of investments that the labor-sending state
engages in to produce new iterations of nationalism and citizenship
prior to migrants' leaving. Ideas of national belonging and notions of
citizens' rights and responsibilities are being transformed in dramatic
ways in countries where governments are invested in the brokerage
of labor.

5

The Philippine Domestic

Gendered Labor, Family, and the Nation-State

When Filipina domestic worker Flor Contemplacion was sentenced to death in 1995 by the Singaporean government for allegedly murdering a fellow Filipina domestic worker and the child in her care, thousands of Filipinos in the Philippines and around the world rallied to demand that the Philippine state stop her impending execution. Protesters believed Contemplacion had been falsely accused. Many thought that Contemplacion had been set up to take the fall for a Singaporean, possibly her employer. The protests were a culmination of many Filipinos' long-standing critiques of the Philippine government's migration program, especially in relation to migrant women workers. Though the state hails migrants as its "new national heroes" churches, scholars, NGOs, as well as grassroots migrant activists in Migrante International, have long contested the government's role in facilitating women's migration as low-wage workers in gender-typed and gender-segregated jobs that make them especially vulnerable to exploitation and sexual abuse.[1] Contemplacion's case exemplified the kinds of vulnerabilities Filipina migrants face at the hands of their employers and ultimately host governments.

The highly publicized and transnational nature of the Contemplacion protests produced a political crisis, one that was critically centered, for the Philippine state. At the height of the crisis the Gancayo Commission, a state-appointed body established to evaluate the impacts of women's migration from the Philippines, came to the following conclusion:

> The saddest reality as found in the mission is the irreparable damage that
> has been inflicted to the reputation of the Filipina woman in the inter-
> national scene because of the indiscriminate deployment of our women
> as domestic helpers (DHs) and entertainers. Our nation has gained the
> embarrassing reputation that we are a country of DHs, entertainers, and
> even prostitutes. . . . It is said that even in a certain dictionary the latest
> definition of the work "Filipina" is a "housemaid."[2]

State officials' own anxieties about women's migration as reflected
in the Gancayo Commission report reveal the degree to which
the state's labor export policy was increasingly being questioned
internally. The notion that Philippine migrants were "new national
heroes" was fast being undermined by the broader public as well as
by government officials themselves.

This chapter's title, "The Philippine Domestic," refers to the
debates in the Philippines regarding the migration of women. These
debates sprung up in the media, churches, and NGOs as well as
among everyday people, particularly in response to women's increasing employment as domestic workers (but also as "entertainers")
overseas. It also refers to the nature of those debates, which centered
on the effects of women's migration on different sets of domestic mat-
ters, namely, family life and the Philippines' national subject-status
on the global stage. These debates were intensified by the death of a
woman migrant worker, widely publicized in a way similar to that
of Contemplacion, that of a twenty-two-year-old Filipina migrant
worker Maricris Sioson. Many of the representations of domestic workers that were produced in response to these two women's
deaths continue to shape how domestic workers are discussed in the
Philippines.

The labor brokerage system is saddled by intrinsic contradictions
that are critically gendered. Eager to supply the world with labor, the
state has inserted migrant women into global circuits of reproductive
labor that separate them from their children (if they are mothers)
and then require that they care for the children of their employers
in faraway destinations.[3] Mothers' absence from the home triggers
"hegemonic national anxiety about the global status of the Filipino
people."[4] Yuval-Davis argues that "a major part of the control of

women as national reproducers relates to their actual biological role as bearers of children."[5] Hence when women cannot perform their biological role of both bearing and caring for their children, the social order on which the nation depends is threatened. As Tadiar suggests, the migration of Filipinas as domestic workers also produces nationalist anxieties because of their hypervisibility as low-wage, low-status workers.[6] The hypervisibility of Filipinas abroad as domestic workers and their invisibility at "home" (that is, the household and the nation-state) raises concerns about the gendered representation of the Philippine nation-state in the global context. Though Filipina migrants work overseas as caregivers to other children, what is more desirable, particularly for the Philippine middle-classes who remain in the Philippines, is that they act as caregivers to their children in their homes in the Philippines.

It is precisely because Filipina migrants care for the children of other nations that middle-class anxieties about the Philippine nation emerge. Filipina women's employment outside the home and, in fact, their employment as domestic workers in the households of more economically privileged classes, is broadly accepted (or perhaps more aptly, expected). It is because Filipina migrants do the work of care for people in other countries and because care work is denigrated that women's employment as domestics abroad becomes problematic and ultimately shameful for the nation-state. These gendered, middle-class contradictions of international migration fed into the protests against the hanging of domestic worker Flor Contemplacion. Migrant grassroots activists were vital to organizing the transnational mobilizations calling for the state's intervention on her behalf and ultimately bringing the state into crisis. However, the anxieties registered by the Philippine middle classes, the church, social reformers, professional NGO activists, and scholars as well as the policy recommendations put forth by these actors appear to have been most decisive in shaping the Migrant Workers and Overseas Filipinos Act of 1995 (RA8042), which was hurriedly introduced and passed in the wake of Contemplacion's hanging. Even if some of these actors were not necessarily central to the policy making process, their orientations toward how the state ought to conduct itself toward migrant women employed as domestics or in other so-called "vulnerable" occupations were homologous with actual policy interventions. RA8042 codified what I have been calling migrant citizenship. This chapter examines the way that gender has shaped migrant citizenship from its inception.

RA8042's "gender-sensitivity" policies specifically aim to resolve gendered anxieties induced by specific kinds of gendered labor migration. The state has introduced a new "gender-sensitive" element into migration, including predeparture educational programs to assist women in making better informed decisions before leaving their families behind. My observations also reveal how these programs attempt to instruct women on how to be better transnational mothers even if they do decide to leave. The state has also enhanced skills training for women destined to work as domestic workers or entertainers because it is believed that "skilled" workers occupy higher status over the "unskilled" in the countries where women are bound to work. Education, in short, is the answer to migrant women's exploitation

In this chapter, I problematize this notion of education. Education as it is understood and implemented by migration officials is structured by logics of neoliberal self-regulation and responsibilization.[7] Anna Guevarra's argument about the state's response to the Contemplacion hanging is correct here. She argues that "the formation of a gendered moral economy around labour migration that links family, religion, and nationalism with capitalist ideals of economic competitiveness and entrepreneurship emerges in this neoliberal framework for managing labour migration."[8] My aim in this chapter is to track the gendered logics that constitute the Philippines' neoliberal migrant citizenship. My aim in this chapter is to track the gendered logics that constitute the Philippines' neoliberal migrant citizenship. The gendered labor of women haunts the Philippine system of labor brokerage even as it is the labor of women that proves to be most profitable for the state. I specifically trace the ways the national polling center Social Weather Stations (SWS) both framed and roused debates about the "Philippine domestic." I am informed here by the "gender knowledge" approach to analyzing migration policy as delineated by Schewenken and Eberhardt.[9] They are concerned with the ways gender knowledge "can become strategic resources in struggles about practices and the construction of reality," especially as it relates to policy making.[10] I am concerned here with how gender knowledge is constructed by SWS, the ways in which that knowledge is inscribed in migration policy, and its consequences for migrant women. Philippine migration policy, especially its "gender-sensitive" policies, very explicitly incorporates gender knowledge. The government deployed its own official studies, like that of the Gancayo Commission cited above, to understand the differences between men's and women's migration experiences. Also at its disposal, however, was gender knowledge produced by institutions like the SWS. While gender knowledge about Filipina migration was prolific and was used by Philippine migration officials, this knowledge relied on problematic assumptions about men's and women's migration. Indeed, much of the gender knowledge about women's migration from the Philippines tended to reify patriarchal understandings and led to state policies and programs aimed at regulating their gender roles and their sexuality and doing so in line with the state's larger commitment to neoliberal labor brokerage.

Contesting Women Migrants' Absence from the Home(land)

By the late 1980s, Filipina international migration began to increase significantly, and by the early 1990s, it rivaled the migration of Filipino men. A majority of these women worked as domestic workers and entertainers. Women's migration from the Philippines, however, is hardly a new phenomenon; women have migrated, most notably as nurses, since the turn of the twentieth century. Moreover, internal migration (that is, rural–urban) has been a key feature of Philippine women's employment since the 1960s.[11]

It was only during the 1990s as women's migration increased in numbers that women migrants began to surpass men. As a greater proportion of women migrants were being deployed to work as entertainers and domestic workers anxieties about the migration of women began to emerge and become increasingly widespread in the Philippines. The media was important in inciting and circulating concerns about women's international migration in the broader public questioning to what extent out-migration was not only detrimental to the women themselves, but to the country as a whole.

The highly publicized death of Filipina migrant worker Maricris Sioson in 1991 was important in initially setting off public discussions about women's out-migration from the Philippines. Sioson, a twenty-two-year-old woman who had worked as an entertainer in Japan, returned to the Philippines dead. Though a Japanese hospital concluded that Sioson had died from hepatitis, it was a conclusion her family did not believe. A second autopsy performed by the Philippines' National Bureau of Investigation (NBI) revealed that Sioson died from traumatic head injuries. In addition, the NBI found stab wounds and cuts in Sioson's vagina.[12]

The conflicting medical reports generated a flurry of news reports. While media response to Sioson's murder focused exclusively on the details of the case, or detailed other women migrants' victimization at the hands of unscrupulous labor recruiters and exploitative employers, some civil society actors, particularly national polling institutes, focused less on sensationalized accounts of women's victimization. Instead, they drew on social scientific methods to analyze broad patterns of women's migration, examining not only its impact on individual women, but on their families and Philippine society at large.[13]

Gendered Migration and the Family

The Social Weather Stations (SWS) were perhaps most critical in beginning to engage the broader national public directly around the issue of women's migration with several sets of surveys after the death of Sioson and leading up to the execution of Contemplacion. While the media certainly played a role in garnering the public's attention to the issue, the SWS's survey research, by its very nature, would draw individual Filipinos into the debate in more immediate ways. Moreover, having gathered data according to the norms of social science, SWS's survey results and analysis could claim the status of "truth" more than information produced by the media.

While the results of the different surveys conducted by the SWS are important, and I discuss them in more detail below, more significant perhaps is how the SWS surveys framed the issue of women and migration and its impact on Filipino families. SWS survey questions about women's migration are both constitutive and reflective of gendered anxieties about women's overseas employment. Feminists have long argued that traditional social scientific methods, including survey research, reproduce dominant gender understandings through both the processes and outcomes of research.[14] The SWS is no exception, as the very questions it asks of respondents are underlined by patriarchal assumptions of women's labor and women's role in the family.

In 1994 a survey entitled "Public Attitudes towards Female Overseas Workers: Implications for Philippine Migration Policy" asked respondents a total of fifteen questions. While the survey attempted to assess how many Filipino families had a member working abroad and how many individuals aspire to overseas employment, a majority of the questions centered on the public's perceptions of Filipina migrants. One of the most notable statements in relation to women migrants and their families that the survey asked respondents to comment on was, "When the mother of the household is working abroad, there are many problems and misunderstandings in the family." Querying whether women's employment outside of the home produces familial problems starts from the assumption that family stability depends on women's presence in the home. While respondents have the opportunity to disagree with the test statement, its very framing relies on the normative assumption that functional (heterosexual) families are those where women work at home.[15]

If the SWS portrayed women's overseas labor as a problem for the Philippine family, actual survey results affirmed the assumptions made by the survey takers. The SWS found that nearly a majority of its twelve hundred respondents, especially those in the higher income brackets, believed that, in fact, the absence of Filipina women from their families produces "many more problems and misunderstandings in the family." The author of the survey report points out, "While many of these issues also directly concern male overseas workers, the debate has singled out overseas working women." This quotation and the survey results illustrate to what extent women's migration specifically is seen by economically privileged Filipinos as especially threatening to family stability. While on the surface it would seem that these "public attitudes" reflect "traditional" notions of men's and women's roles in the family, these "attitudes," in fact, run counter to the high prevalence of Filipinas' employment outside the home,[16] whether it is to work abroad, to work in other distant locations in the Philippines, or to work in factories or on farms. In the next section, it will become clear that what is really at stake here is less women's absence from the home per se, but their presence as low-wage and low-status workers in other nations.

Gendered Migration and the Philippine Nation

Alongside concerns about the consequences of women's migration for their families were concerns about the consequences of women's migration on the nation more broadly. In the same "Public Attitudes" survey, the SWS also asked respondents to what extent they agreed or disagreed with the test statement, "Women working abroad bring shame to our country."[17] That next to questions on women's migration and family was a question on national shame relates to McClintock's argument that "nations are frequently figured through the iconography of familial and domestic space."[18] The questions on the "Public Attitude" survey rest on the logic that women's employment as low-wage, low-status workers has negative implications for the global representation of the Philippine nation-state.

The "Public Attitudes" survey results revealed that there was little consensus among respondents across gender, class, and region, yet the SWS came to the following conclusion:

> On the statement that women workers overseas bring shame to the country, the predominant position is disagreement (47 percent). Still, the percentages who outright agree (21 percent) and those who neither agree nor disagree (32 percent) are, uncomfortably high.

Figure 20. Ninoy Aquino International Airport, 2008. Photograph by Ben Razon. Source: Sugar Mountain Media.

By discussing the findings in this way, SWS effectively colludes in producing women's migration as a national shame even as the "objective" figures do not indicate that the feeling of nationalist shame is widespread. It can be argued that the SWS's findings reveal that most people (79 percent) either do not believe that women's migration is shameful or are ambivalent, even as they may be concerned about its effects on families. Yet the SWS concludes that people's sense of shame is "uncomfortably" high. By highlighting the uncomfortable "fact" of nationalist shame, the SWS ultimately produces it as an issue.

Radcliffe notes how "social identities, including national identities, are constituted through relations of intersubjectivity, that is, the (partial) internalization of others' images of oneself."[19] Survey respondents' (and survey researchers') beleaguered sense of nationalism is shaped by this intersubjective process but within an international

arena. It is because Filipina migrants care for the children of other
nations as low-status domestic workers that classed anxieties about
the Philippine nation emerge.

Vulnerable Women and the Paternal State

If the SWS survey constituted and reflected gendered notions of
women's labor in families and constructions of Philippine nationalism
in a global context, they also produced specific kinds of gendered
understandings of the state's relationship and responsibilities toward
women migrants.

The 1994 "Public Attitudes" survey report states:

> The character of female emigration has changed. There are many more
> young and single women, originating from further flung Philippine prov-
> inces. Hired as housemaids, singers, and dancers, these women work at
> jobs that are inherently difficult, dangerous, and are unprotected by labor
> law in many receiving countries.

In this quotation, migrant women are characterized as innocent,
young, and nubile. The report appears to suggest that because the
profile of migrant women is younger and more rural than previous
cohorts of women migrants (namely, migrant nurses) they therefore
have less control over their migration decisions because they lack
experience and skills.

These infantilizing constructions of Filipina migrants are aimed
at compelling the state to respond with migration reform. They
rely, however, on specific gendered logics. Because women choos-
ing employment abroad do so either out of youthful and/or rural
ignorance or as a consequence of deficiencies in their values systems,
they ultimately require intervention by the paternal state to prevent
them from harming their families and the nation. Whether women
lack moral gumption or are simply too young to know better, the
state must assume better paternal custody over them. It must control
its innocent, if sometimes wayward, daughters.

State actors, however, were initially ambivalent about the gendered debates produced and circulated by the media and national
polling groups like the SWS and continued to be fairly ambivalent

when the Flor Contemplacion case first erupted in public protests. In a policy analysis produced by the Department of Labor and Employment in response to the initial news about Contemplacion's imminent hanging, it states:

> It is the exception to the norm that makes the news, and in recent days we have been flooded with media accounts of the travails of some of our overseas workers. But the truth is that only a very few — less than one thousand — of all our migrant workers ever get into trouble. The great majority are an unalloyed benefit both to their host countries and to their homeland.[20]

Here the state characterizes Contemplacion's case, and other similar cases, as being anomalous. Moreover, state officials believed that communist insurgency would have greater impact on the Philippines:

> At present the country is reeling from the political fallout of the Flor Contemplacion case.... Against these headaches, however, there is one major political benefit that is well-nigh incalculable. And this is that overseas employment — in mopping up part of our labor surplus — provides for greater political and social stability in the country. One study of the effect of the OCW program on the Communist insurgency notes that the program has deprived the movement of many recruits. And the misery index, which the insurgents count on, has been immeasurably affected by the remittances of OCWs to their families and their communities.[21]

Here the state has an understanding of the Filipino family and national stability that diverges from broader public discussions. Whereas in public debates Filipino families and the nation are destabilized by the absence of women, for the state, the presence of remittances in the family is what secures the nation's stability. Families are the nation's bulwark against the more menacing threat of communism.

Eventually, however, the state was compelled to respond to the protests against Contemplacion's hanging, which were expanding far beyond the Philippines. It is perhaps precisely because debates about the Filipina domestic spilled over into the international arena with the globalization of migrants' protests that the state felt especially obliged to finally act. As Tadiar argues, "Regulating the export of Filipino maids is really about gaining control over the Philippine production of labour for the global community, and thereby asserting the nation's agency and subjectivity in the eyes of the world."[22] It can be argued that the Philippine state was figuratively emasculated in the international arena because it could not prevent the execution of one of its citizens, a woman no less. Introducing so-called "gendered-sensitive" migration reforms can be understood as a state strategy to recuperate its gendered national subject status and not a measure to address the very real abuse and exploitation faced by women (and men) workers abroad.

Republic Act 8042 (RA8042), passed very soon after the execution of Flor Contemplacion, mandated many policies very specifically related to better "protecting" women migrants. RA8042 appears to directly incorporate the sorts of reforms advocated in SWS documents over the years. For instance RA8042 declares that "the State recognizes that the ultimate protection to all migrant workers is the possession of skills. Pursuant to this and as soon as practicable, the government shall deploy and/or allow the deployment only to skilled Filipino workers." For domestic workers, officially categorized as "vulnerable workers," this has meant mandatory skills training programs prior to deployment overseas. In addition to this skills training, the state also expanded its predeployment worker education programs, to better disseminate "information of labor and employment conditions, migration realities and other facts, and adherence of particular countries to international standards on human and workers' rights which will adequately prepare individuals for making informed and intelligent decisions about overseas employment." Postdeployment, in countries of destination, RA8042 mandates government services at the Philippines' embassies or consular offices, including additional training and skills upgrading programs. The state provides legal and welfare services for migrant workers in distress. Because the state has officially incorporated a "gender sensitive" approach to migration policy, it means that all of these programs attempt to address the specific problems faced by migrant women. However, appeals for increased state protections for women like "gender-sensitive" policies, as Wendy Brown points out, "involve seeking protection *from* masculinist institutions *against* men, a move more in keeping with the politics of feudalism than freedom."[23]

A critical assessment of the state's "gender-sensitive" policies along with an analysis of interviews of migration officials several years after RA8042 was passed, reveals how migration reform is ultimately less about the regulation of women's migration or even "protection" and more about the regulation of women migrants themselves. The programs created by RA8042 are mainly focused on migrants' education and "decision-making" and therefore deflect attention from the state's role in actually (re)producing ideas of Filipinas' docility as part of its labor brokerage strategy. Filipinas' vulnerability is arguably a consequence of the racializing and gendering "marketing" practices of the Philippine state. At the same time, by categorizing only specific kinds of overseas jobs as "vulnerable" the state obscures the fact that foreign employment, by its very nature (as "flexible," contractualized, and temporary) renders all migrants fundamentally vulnerable. The ways the bureaucrats and other state officials attempt to regulate migrant women echoes the very same gendered ideas that the public as reported by SWS employed in their calls for migration reform.

A migration official in the POEA explains the purpose of women workers' training, as well as their education through the Pre-Departure Orientation Seminar (PDOS): "Our concern is that often these workers do not send money to the Philippines or don't try to take care of family problems at home. These kinds of seminars emphasize workers' responsibilities to their families." A very high-ranking official of the POEA explains that the state must provide domestic workers and entertainers specific kinds of programs because "there are lots of social costs when a mother or elder sister is missing."

For state authorities, migration programs actively cultivate women's sense of familial responsibility. The assumption that officials make is that women are not already orienting themselves to their families' needs. As a consequence of women's lack of familial duty, families suffer a number of "social costs." If the SWS pointed to increasing problems in migrant women's family lives as a means for calling for migration reform, bureaucrats attempt to address these problems by trying to inculcate certain kinds of family values among migrant women.

If there were calls for the state to assume better (paternal) custody of migrant women, it was clear in my other interviews of officials
that these paternal/parental understandings about state–citizen relations characterized their own views. In an interview with the highest
ranking official of the POEA, who began to weep profusely during
the course of our discussion, she states:

> We really need to take care of them. When I see the DH [domestic
> helpers] and the OPAs [overseas performing artists], I just cry. They're
> so innocent.... I really hope things change for them. We really have to
> reach out to them, to give them self-respect and confidence.... You know,
> when we are on the airplane or in the airport traveling, when we have
> them next to us, deep inside we're ashamed.

Here this official uses familial language in describing the state's role
in regulating women's migration. The state, in her words, must "take
care of" domestic workers and entertainers because they are "innocent." By doing so, she suggests, the state will not only equip them
with the ability to better negotiate the challenges of working overseas, but that the state may be able to deal with the deep-seated
sense of nationalist shame women's migration produces.

As I discuss above, one the most important aspects of RA8042
is that it consolidates predeparture programs for women workers.
Observations of the programmatic measures instituted to fulfill this
mandate reveal how initiatives meant to "protect" women workers are a means of disciplining them to perform specific familial
and nationalist obligations. This is most clear in the Pre-Departure
Orientation Seminar (PDOS).

Predeparture education has been a component of the Philippines' overseas migration program since the institutionalization of the
POEA. The POEA even has its own "Workers Education Division,"
which has been actively engaged in enacting a variety of policies and
programs, in addition to the PDOS, aimed at helping prospective
migrants to make "more informed" decisions. The official I interviewed explained that many of her colleagues worried that the PDOS
did not adequately influence people's behavior. She described how
the POEA was investing heavily in identifying pedagogical styles that
could be more effective. The idea is that people hoping to work

abroad need to fully understand the challenges that employment abroad entails, including potentially difficult working conditions and having to negotiate with an unfamiliar culture. In fact, attendance at a PDOS is a mandatory predeparture requirement and prospective migrants must provide proof of having attended a seminar before being cleared for overseas employment. Predeparture education programs are seen as especially important and even "empowering" for "vulnerable" categories of women migrants.

Though the PDOS is generally given by migrants' recruitment agencies, the POEA requires that to be employed as domestic helpers or entertainers women migrants can take the PDOS only at the POEA or through an officially registered NGO. According to an official, "vulnerable workers...are required to take their PDOS at the POEA and with NGOs where they can learn about their rights as opposed to going to agencies who will teach them to be docile."

The PDOS is a full-day activity that covers a range of topics including migrants' employment rights and a so-called "values formation" session, my focus here. Most of the attendees are women bound for employment as domestic helpers or entertainers. Many, however, both women and men, are there to fulfill their PDOS requirements because they sought employment not through recruitment agencies but through personal networks or direct contact with foreign employers. In one of the PDOS sessions I attended, a female instructor in her early thirties with a kindly demeanor began her session on migrants' rights with an interactive activity on "confidence building." The official at the Workers Education Division whom I interviewed indicated that she favored this instructor for her "nontraditional" teaching methods, which includes class participation and group activities.

In the "confidence building" exercise, students are asked to pick a partner and to introduce themselves to one another. They seem to enjoy the exercise as everyone engages in animated conversation. Some excitedly share how they will be going to work abroad for the very first time; some "rehires," meanwhile, enumerate all the countries where they have been employed and describe what it is like to work in those different places. The instructor then calls on individuals to share what they have learned about their partners, pressing them to remember as many details about their partners as they can. Some have a difficult time remembering their partner's first names. Others scramble to remember points from their own conversation in case they get called upon. After a few more teams are called upon, the instructor explains the point of the exercise: that first impressions between people are important, and even more so between workers and their employers. The best way to make a good first impression with one's employer, she then suggests, is to "(1) speak clearly and (2) be assertive. When you face your employer for the first time, speak clearly and loudly. What impression do you think you'll make? That you are confident and intelligent."

The instructor then asks workers to stand up and share what they learned from the exercise. Several workers raise their hands immediately to be called upon. One woman struggles to explain in English, "To be good OFWs, we need to be able ... [she continues in Tagalog] ... we should be confident in ourselves in facing our employers." Another woman states, also in Tagalog, "We shouldn't be hesitant about asking for instructions." Yet another woman gets up to speak, saying in Tagalog, "Even if you don't like the work, you should do it."

Yet "confidence," as the PDOS instructor and the students define it, is paradoxically about being good and ultimately compliant workers. For the instructor, one must face one's employer with confidence in order to create a good impression, and workers concur that to be "good OFWs" one must be confident. According to some, to be confident is to be able to ask for instructions on how to do work properly, and to be confident is to work even if one does not enjoy it. Here we see some of the logics that actually underlie this ostensibly "empowering" PDOS. Reminiscent of the "self-esteem" programs launched in the state of California analyzed by Barbara Cruikshank, the PDOS's "confidence-building" exercises are neoliberal techniques of self-government and regulation. "Confidence" becomes a means by which one strengthens one's will to accept adverse conditions rather than challenging them. To do so is to be a good overseas worker; indeed, it is to be a good overseas *Filipino* worker and there-fore to take up the mantle of Philippine migrant citizenship. As Cruikshank argues, "Democratic government, even self-government, depends upon the ability of citizens to recognize, isolate, and act upon their own subjectivity, to be governors of their selves."[24]

The disciplinary function of the PDOS becomes more appar-ent when the instructor launches into a discussion of the nature of contractual employment. She talks about the terms of migrants' employment contracts in fuller detail, illustrating the kinds of pro-tections the POEA has instituted to make certain that workers are guaranteed fair working and living conditions in their countries of employment. The instructor even explains how the state engages in bilateral and multilateral agreements with labor-receiving coun-tries so that they guarantee rights to Filipino migrant workers. The instructor notes too how the Philippine state is a signatory to the U.N. Convention on Migrant Workers' Rights.

The instructor's account of workers' rights as guaranteed in their employment contracts prompts discussion among the workers; some point to the Philippine government as responsible for undesirable contractual terms. A woman who had worked in a hospital in Saudi Arabia talked about how she had signed a contract for a specific salary as a staff nurse, but instead she was relegated to work as a menial laborer in the hospital. She complained about it to the hospital managers and was luckily able to get the staff position and a higher wage. This prompts another woman who had also worked in Saudi Arabia, as a nurse, to stand up and challenge the statement made by the first woman. A debate then ensues. The second nurse states irately, "It's a problem that starts here in the Philippines," arguing that the problem does not have to do with the employer, but with the Philippine government. Other workers start to talk among themselves and chuckle in agreement. "Nigerians and Indians get better wages for less skills!" she exclaims angrily.

The instructor responds that the wage rates depend on several fac-tors including work experience, but she concedes that other nationals do not get the same rates as Filipinos and that theirs may be better. She explains, "Our country isn't always able to get better agreements, but it's also about labor demand and supply. On the other hand, in Taiwan you can hire two Thais for the work of one Filipino. This is true also on the ships. Why? Because they accept it. But what do you want?" she asks. "Increased wages for fewer jobs or decreased wages for more to be able to leave? That's our struggle with migration management," she explains. The instructor attempts to downplay the role of the state in setting the terms of the employment contract, despite workers' insistence that the state is accountable for their wage rates. She suggests that the Philippine state has little power to negotiate with other states over wages. Even if the state were able to secure better wages, it runs the risk of losing overseas jobs for its citizens. In short, workers must accept the work they have and be compliant workers.

What is significant about these exchanges between workers and the PDOS instructor is that, first, it becomes clear that migrants believe the state must intervene to negotiate better terms of employment on their behalf. Indeed, RA8042 has been hailed as the Magna Carta of Philippine migrant's rights. Yet in the PDOS, migrants are taught to accept the terms of employment they already have because they run the risk of losing their jobs if they make too many demands. This PDOS, however, does give workers a space to express their concerns about being exploited overseas. The PDOS instructor is able to manage the outrage expressed by workers, affirming that workers can cope with their problems by "confidently" addressing their employers. At the same time, however, she makes it clear to workers that ultimately the Philippine state is limited in its power to protect them. Even though she explains how the Philippine government works to ensure that workers enjoy protections through the certification of the employment contract and even through bilateral and multilateral agreements, she simultaneously asserts that the Philippine state is weak. The resolution workers are left with, ultimately, is to accept their conditions; otherwise they face the prospect of unemployment.

Despite these critiques of the government, most of the other workers in this seminar seem to concur with the instructor that the state cannot be responsible for unequal employment conditions and that ultimately one should not take issue with these inequalities. One woman's final words in response to the discussion of unequal wages were: "You can't always compare [your wages with the wages of other nationalities] because it causes problems in the workplace."

Following the session on employment contracts comes the session on "values formation." For this section the instructor is an elderly woman who introduces herself as a nun who had previously worked for a nongovernmental organization advocating migrant workers' rights. She takes a very different approach from the first instructor, whom I describe above, relying less on discussion and more on conventional lecturing, though with a liberal dose of humor. Workers are just as attentive to this instructor, laughing, sometimes uncomfortably, at all of the crude jokes she makes early on in her part of the seminar.

She states, "Filipinos suffer from a cancer, a cancer that starts here and that we take with us abroad, a cancer that needs to be cured even before you leave. Values, priorities, beliefs, attitudes: this is defective in the Pinoy." She proceeds to joke about the various cultural "defects" Filipinos suffer from, including overzealous consumption, materialism, and gambling. People laugh in agreement as she describes images of Filipino migrants weighed down with baggage full of goodies purchased overseas for their relatives or at airport duty-free shops when they return from work overseas. When she jokes about how the Filipino is the magna cum laude in *pusoy,* a card game, even teaching foreigners to play, the students find it hilarious.

Her tone, however, starts to change dramatically from being funny to admonishing: "We're like this. We blow our money. But the fact is these jobs aren't always plentiful. There are limits, and we're at the finishing line. . . . You have to compete with cheaper labor." The room all of a sudden falls silent, and people shift uncomfortably in their seats. She continues with a moralizing tirade:

> You have your objective of achieving a "better life," but what are your concrete plans? Food? Shelter? Clothing? Education? What about your value systems? If you rely on the Pinoy value system will you succeed? It is not clear that you will. Food, clothing, education, will only deal with your physical needs. There is something else that's important, more than the

> dollars you send. There's the spiritual aspect. Remember, as OFWs, you
> are Pinoy and you're Christian. *Bayan, lipunan, pamilia* [Nation, society,
> family]. These aspects are within us but who is it that brings all sorts
> of problems to other countries? We do. It is embarrassing. Look at our
> country. Our heroes are dead and rotting. Take care of the dignity of your
> country.

In the instructor's invectives, we see family, religion, and nation
intertwined as a means of governing the behavior of migrant workers.
The instructor aims to discourage the unproductive use of one's wages
overseas. What is important is that migrants are to send their money
back home to their families in the Philippines and not to waste it on
leisure or luxury items. Consumerism, according to this instructor, is
a vice much like gambling and is ultimately immoral. The instructor
claims moral authority early in the session by identifying herself as a
nun, and it is an authority that workers appear to accept.

While problematic consumerism or even gambling may affect
migrants' families, the instructor suggests that these behaviors also
have consequences for the nation more broadly. She insists that
Filipino migrants are embodiments of the nation abroad and to
ideally represent the nation requires that migrants be morally upright
individuals, refraining from behavior that may sully the image of
the Philippines overseas. There are penalties for those who fail
to exhibit nationalism and Catholic morality. After lamenting the
"defectiveness" of Filipino values, the PDOS instructor warned
workers:

> First, going abroad is not the same as it used to be. You're faced with
> problems that the government can't control. For example, your jobs are
> not always guaranteed. In Malaysia, jobs for Filipinos were stopped. The
> same is true for Taiwan. You're competing now with cheaper workers. You
> want better wages and you deserve it but they are willing to work much
> cheaper.

She continued, "Let's just work." Being morally upright representatives of the nation, therefore, ultimately means being good and docile
workers. To be otherwise is to ultimately threaten the nation-state,
which loses global labor markets to competitors.

Throughout the instructor's diatribe, workers are still and quiet, many with their heads bowed, almost in shame. Even I had a difficult time looking up at her or even looking at the other people in the room. The message clearly had an effect on everyone. Perhaps it is because she is a nun, or that she draws on religious and nationalist sentiment that makes her presentation especially effective.

When the "values formation" instructor bemoans the defectiveness of Filipino culture, she is especially worried about Filipina migrant women's sexuality:

> More and more Filipinas are becoming pregnant before getting married. They are having sex as often as they change clothes. Nowadays the wedding march is "here comes the bride, six months inside." . . . Even when a Filipina attends mass, she's dressed so sexy that instead of "body of Christ," the priest says, "Wow, what a body!"

Filipina women are "culturally defective" because they are sexually promiscuous — a problem that they bring with them when they go overseas so that the Philippines have a "reputation." She states:

> When you ask in different countries what a Pinay is they will say domestic helper or fucking machine. Men in other countries will actually try their luck on Filipinas, but you don't have to give in! They'll actually respect your decision not to give in, but because we have only money-values, we give in.

This remark suggests that Filipinas are not just sexually promiscuous; their promiscuity is linked to having "money-values," that is, women are willing to prostitute themselves for money because their values are misplaced. Yet paradoxically the Philippines actively trains women to work as "entertainers" overseas, which requires them to perform highly sexualized dance routines so that they can earn lucrative salaries overseas. In the very same building, women hoping to be entertainers are judged by a panel that includes a POEA representative in a Pre-Departure Showcase Preview. Dancers were often scantily clad and performed provocative moves. In the PDOS, however, the state attempts to define the limits of migrant women's sexuality to ensure that the Philippine state's representation on the global stage is not significantly undermined even as their sexuality is necessary to their overseas employment and ultimately their remittances (off the job, for entertainers, and on the job, for domestic workers).[25] It is specifically the unruly sexual conduct of women migrants that are problematic for the state.

One means of being respectable women is through maintaining their roles as mothers. The instructor states:

> You'll be faced with loneliness, worry, anxiety, and homesickness. Given all these challenges, ask yourself if you can handle it physically, emotionally, and spiritually. Through it all, remember your family. Some people deal with these problems with sex, but you need to remember what our role is with God. Sex is supposed to be for procreation in a family.

Here, as Guevárra observes, the state "not only endeavours to make them into economically productive workers but also ensures that they are 'good' wives, mothers, and women. Normative gender roles thus define the moral grounds upon which Filipino women must fashion themselves as workers."[26]

If women migrants bring shame to the nation, they may ultimately cause problems for future migrants. As the instructor of PDOS's "values formation" section contends, should "bad" workers or problematic women workers tarnish the Philippines' image, all categories of Filipino migrants may lose future opportunities for overseas work. "It's in your hands," she says, "the image of this country and the prospects for your fellow Filipinos."

Conclusion

International migration has become an important developmental strategy in the Philippines as the state benefits from the millions of dollars in remittances generated yearly by its citizens employed abroad. Specifically, women migrants have come to play an increasingly significant role as overseas workers. Women's migration in particularly, however, has become a critical site for national debate as people in the Philippines, especially the middle classes, have contested expected meanings of gender as it has been transformed by international migration.

Different civil society actors have been concerned with the negative consequences of women's migration, including the extreme forms of violence and abuse women suffer while working and living abroad, and have attempted to advocate migration reform. Research produced by the SWS to support demands for reform, however, reify problematic, ultimately patriarchal, notions of femininity. It characterizes women's migration as undermining the social and moral fabric of the Filipino family and ultimately the Philippine nation-state.

The state, though initially ambivalent about national(istic) anxieties about women's migration, even with the highly graphic and violent death of Maricris Sioson, is ultimately compelled to address them, particularly when migrants in the labor diaspora brought the issue of women's migration to a global stage with the protests against the hanging of domestic worker Flor Contemplacion. When the Philippine state finds its gendered subject status tested in the global arena, it finally responds to the broader calls for migration policy reform. It incorporates many of the same representations as are circulated by key knowledge producers like the SWS in its construction of new migration laws. Yet the paternal logics on which demands for migration reform rest have led not to the increased regulation of the state's migration apparatus, but to the regulation of migrant women themselves. Citizenship, as promised through RA8042, is critically gendered. Moreover, debates about the "Philippine domestic" reveal how tenuous the Philippine labor brokerage system truly is.

6

Migrant Workers' Rights?

Regulating Remittances
and Repatriation

In May 2001, nearly seven hundred Filipina and Filipino workers employed at sister garment factories producing clothing for U.S. retailers such as the Gap and Old Navy went on a wildcat strike. They demanded higher wages as well as fair compensation for their piece-rate and overtime work. Though the strike involved Philippine workers, it did not take place in any of the Philippines' export-processing zones: it took place in Brunei, a neighboring country. Philippine migrants enlisted the assistance of the Brunei-based Philippine embassy and consular officers in negotiating a settlement between themselves, their Malaysian-Chinese employers, the Brunei government, and their Philippine-based labor recruitment agencies. Philippine embassy officials would eventually stand in for workers during negotiations. Even the vice president of the Philippines became involved. When many of the workers refused to accept management's counteroffer, agreed on by the Philippine government, Philippine officials facilitated their repatriation and encouraged the almost three hundred repatriated migrants to file claims against their Philippine-based recruitment agencies through state bureaucracies that regulate overseas employment. And they did. But the claims process was incredibly daunting. In a tragic and unexpected twist, the workers actually found themselves subject to counterclaims by the recruitment agencies that had sent them to Brunei, which accused the workers of having violated the terms of their contracts. When I left the field in

116

September 2001, the claims process was at an impasse and the once militant workers seemed resigned to never getting compensation.

The nature of the strike, the role of the Philippine state in the negotiations process, and its outcome make this struggle a good illustration of the limits of Philippine migrant "citizenship." This case demonstrates the contradictory nature of the labor brokerage state's relationship with its overseas citizens given its interests in sustaining outflows of labor. Since the massive outcry over the hanging of domestic worker Flor Contemplacion, the Philippine government has had to explicitly spell out mechanisms by which it pledges to safeguard worker's interests. The Philippine government needed to placate its citizens' clamor for migration policy reforms through the passage of RA8042. A cursory examination of the Philippine government's migration policies as contained in RA8042 and other documents indicates that the state offers a wide range of programs meant to ensure migrants' employment protections. In Figure 21, I summarize kinds of employment protections, welfare programs, and other services the Philippine state ostensibly offers to migrants both in the Philippines and overseas. The summary is based on my interviews with officials and studies of policy documents.

The Philippines' global labor trade, however, relies on stable diplomatic relations with labor-receiving governments. These relations depend on the Philippine state's ability to make certain that Philippine migrants comply with the customs and laws of their host countries, and ultimately the Philippine state must be able to guarantee that workers meet the expectations of their employers. The contradictions between the Philippine state's role as a labor broker and as protector of its citizens becomes clear in this labor struggle.

Brunei in particular has been an important market for Philippine migrants and has counted among the top ten destinations for Philippine workers in Asia for nearly a decade. Brunei's garment industry is relatively new for this oil-rich Southeast Asian country. Employers in Brunei's garment industry, however, rely on short-term, foreign migrant workers as locals shun low-wage, low-status factory jobs.

Employment Protection Programs

In the Philippines (predeparture):

- POEA-certified overseas employment contract compliant with Philippine labor laws
- Grievance mechanisms through POEA or NLRC

Overseas:

- Bilateral agreements on employment protections (DFA)
- Grievance mechanisms through embassy and consular offices and/or ILAS representative

Welfare Services and Programs

In the Philippines (predeparture):

- General predeparture education programs (POEA)
- Women-specific predeparture programs (POEA)
- Programs and services for families (OWWA)

Overseas:

- Social activities, legal assistance, and other programs and services at embassies and consular offices

Figure 21. Employment protections and welfare programs.

Both Brunei and the Philippines, like other Southeast Asian states, engage in what Aihwa Ong calls graduated sovereignty:

> Citizens in zones that are differently articulated to global production and financial circuits are subjected to different kinds of surveillance and in practice enjoy different sets of civil, political, and economic rights. By thus calibrating its control over sovereignty to the challenges of global capital, the so-called tiger-state developed a system of graduated zones that also protects against pockets of political unrest.[1]

What this case reveals is that graduated sovereignties, particularly when they involve multiple states, as is true with international migration, require negotiations between countries. Labor-receiving and labor-sending states must work out compromises that preserve their interests and ultimately the interests of foreign capital, even as they manage to contain potential strife among their respective populations.

In the first major section of this chapter, I look closely at the employment and welfare protections that the Philippine state is putatively committed to extending to migrant workers through laws like RA8042. I specifically focus on the mechanisms by which the government is supposed to ensure that migrants' employment contracts comply with Philippine labor standards and the procedures by which migrants can file grievances against contractual violations. In the second section I explore the negotiations process in the Brunei labor struggle, paying close attention in particular to contestations over the interpretations of Philippine migrants' employment contracts. It is the employment contract that entangles a Philippine migrant, a foreign employer, the host state, and the Philippine state in a complex set of relations. The contract is a meaningful document to Philippine migrants who refer to it to justify their wage demands and their enlistment of Philippine government representatives to represent their interests during the negotiations process. It is also where the graduated sovereignties of two states potentially collide.

What is revealed in this strike is that the bureaucratic processing the Philippine state institutes to ensure that Philippine migrants' contracts conform to national wage and employment standards is ultimately invalid outside the Philippines. Though the contract is supposed to govern and regulate the relations between employers and migrant workers, the migrants' contract's applicability and validity depend on its recognition in a country of employment. Moreover, though Philippine migration officials are mandated to protect their citizens and to advocate on their behalf, their ability to do so is constrained by the sovereignty of host states, the interests of foreign employers, and the Philippine state's own interests in maintaining a presence in particular labor markets.

Philippine migrants, however, are entitled to return to the Philippines to pursue their grievances against their employers if all grievance mechanisms overseas have been exhausted (assuming there are any); it is an option that half of the striking workers pursue. The third major section of this chapter explores workers' experiences as they negotiate with the grievance machinery back home. I consider migrants' different claims-making strategies. I find that some workers attempt to sustain their collective unity and try to assert their demands outside of the prescribed grievance mechanisms, but they ultimately lose steam. Others, however, rely on the state's grievance machinery as well as the assistance of state-sanctioned legal services, but their claims seem to be stalled in the morass of the bureaucracy. Workers' unsuccessful grievance claims make plain the limitations of Philippine migrants' "citizenship."

I end with a discussion of President Gloria Macapagal-Arroyo's state visit to Brunei, which took place shortly after the workers' strike. During the visit, it became clear that her purpose was to smooth over relations with the government of Brunei and thereby keep it as a "client." The imperatives of labor brokerage prevailed in the end.

Employment Protections

Following the passage of RA8042 in 1995, the POEA's most recent *Rules and Regulations* mandates that migrants' employment contracts set a floor for migrants' wages that is presumably fair for Philippine citizens working overseas.

> guaranteed wages for regular work and overtime pay, as appropriate, which shall not be lower than the prescribed minimum wage in the host country, not lower than the appropriate minimum wage set forth in a bilateral agreement or international convention duly ratified by the host country and the Philippines or not lower than the minimum wage in the Philippines, whichever is highest.[2]

According to migration officials, the POEA even coordinates with their overseas counterparts at ILAS as well as with the diplomatic corps to verify that the firms that secure labor from Philippine-based recruiters are legitimate and that the working and living conditions provided by them meet a minimum set of requirements as determined by the DOLE in the Philippines. Foreign employers are supposed to offer working and living conditions that are similar to if not better than those considered acceptable in the Philippines. Philippine migration officials abroad actually conduct site visits to ensure migrants' living conditions are adequate. Meanwhile, prior to the migrants' departure through the migration bureaucracy the POEA certifies that their employment contracts are in order. At Manila's Ninoy Aquino International Airport migrant workers must show their certified contracts to POEA representatives before boarding a plane.

Employment contracts certified by the Philippine government specify grievance procedures for contractual violations:

> All claims and complaints relative to the employment contract of the employee shall be settled in accordance with Company policies, rules and regulations. In case the Employee contests the decision of the Employer, the matter shall be settled amicably with the participation of the Labor Attache or any authorized representative of the Philippine Embassy/Consulate nearest to the site of employment.[3]

According to a POEA official, the Philippine government even sends representatives to different countries to conduct "welfare missions" to attend to cases of worker abuse such as overwork and contractual violations.

If contractual disputes between migrants and their employers cannot be resolved amicably while workers are overseas, the Philippine government allows migrant workers to file monetary claims against their employers upon their return to the Philippines. As stated in RA8042:

> The POEA or the NLRC [Nationalism Labor Relations Commission] shall have original and exclusive jurisdiction over any administrative and disciplinary cases and all disputes or controversies arising out of or by virtue of this Contract. All rights and obligations of the parties to this Contract, shall be governed by the laws of the Republic of the Philippines, international conventions, treaties and covenants wherein the Philippines is a signatory.

The POEA has an Adjudication Branch, which facilitates mediation processes between migrants and their Philippine-based recruitment agencies with a specific focus on recruitment violations (for example, the recruitment agency posts an employment ad for one type of job but migrants discover that they are actually performing a different kind of job). The National Labor Relations Commission, however, handles money claims migrant workers may have against their recruitment agencies or their employers.

As the latter portion of the employment contract provision cited above indicates, bilateralism is a mechanism by which the Philippine state pledges to ensure workers' protections. This was a point many officials emphasized in my interviews. In fact, the Philippine government has successfully negotiated social security benefits for Philippine migrants through bilateral agreements with Austria, France, Italy, Spain, and the U.K. and at the time of my research it was apparently negotiating similar benefits with Denmark, Greece, Sweden, and Switzerland. According to one POEA official, the Philippines has even attempted to work with other labor-sending states to collectively negotiate with specific host countries for better working conditions for all of their migrants:

> Philippine labor attaches abroad were working with Vietnam, India, and Sri Lanka along with other labor-exporting countries to make collective recommendations about protections for workers in Korea. The plan was that labor-exporting countries should develop a collective voice with regard to various migrant workers' issues vis-à-vis labor-importing countries.

That these employment protections actually serve workers' interests, however, is quite dubious, as is evident in the Philippine migrants' labor struggle in Brunei.

Competing Contracts

The month of April 2001 was especially grueling for the Filipina and Filipino workers employed in the Malanei garment factories in Brunei's export processing zones.[4] Workers were not just working overtime; they were working *overnight* to meet production quotas. Yet when they received their monthly paycheck for the month of April in early May (they are paid only on a monthly basis), their wages were no higher than their March wages. According to Tessie,

Figure 22. Factory compound in Brunei, 2001. Photograph by Melissa Alipalo.

> The workers were very depressed because the wages were so low; we wondered why since last March there wasn't as much overtime yet our salary for [April] was even lower and we worked overnight and there was always overtime.

The workers felt cheated and devised a plan to present their concerns to management. It was decided that on the following Monday they would not punch in their time cards and would not work. They would simply sit at their sewing machines until management agreed to discuss the workers' list of demands and grievances. The workers' decision on what course of action to take was influenced in part by the measures taken by their Bangladeshi coworkers. Like the Filipinos, the Bangladeshis were employed as temporary foreign workers in Brunei. However, unlike the Filipino migrants, they were predominantly men. They were able to secure a raise from the management only after damaging a boss's car. The Filipinas believed that a work stoppage and discussions would be more effective in getting management to address their demands. Submitted to the management in a handwritten letter, the demands were as follows:

We, workers of Malaynei Garments and Textiles factory, has united together and requesting about salary increase. Instead of the said salary, we would like to turn it into $320 (Brunei dollars). Reasons:

1. We are all aware that factories here in Brunei, workers received B$320 for their basic.

2. Bangladeshi workers came here in Brunei were trainee sewers only. Unlike Philippines, they came here for worked, were skilled already. So why is it that they've got same salaries and they've got an salary increase.

We have also requests and demands regarding factory:

1. We already requested to have an Orbic fan at the middle of sewing area. Because workers cannot concentrate more in the sewing cause of too much hot that cause skin allergies and got sick.

2. *We wanted also that what contract stated must be applied.*

3. We wanted also to have a copy or we would like to know the computation of our salary.

4. Why is it that the prices of the dress we sewing instead of increasing it decreased (costs).

5. Then one thing is overtime, we've noticed that we worked for a long hour of time. But why is it that some of our overtime not yet included in payroll.

6. About our lending money before we go here (Brunei) we pay 15,000 pesos and B$1,720 cut every month to the agent. It is obviously very high and besides our salary computation not followed instead of basic (daily) it become dozen rated.

7. *About salaries, we would like to receive it every 7th day of the month. Not 15th day because it stated in contract.*

8. Well this is all about. We are hoping for your kind consideration and granting our request. Thank you very much. (Emphases added)

The Philippine migrants' primary demand was for a wage increase. As the workers explained to me, in addition to demanding a wage increase, they wanted the employer to comply with the piece-rate and overtime rate spelled out in their employment contracts. In the list of demands submitted by the workers to management as quoted above, workers cite their employment contracts when they make their claims.

Based on their interpretation of the contract, workers believed that as long as they met the monthly production quotas set by their employers, they would be paid a monthly wage of B$260 (or the equivalent of $143.03). Additionally, they believed that they could earn more money by earning piece-rates for every item of clothing completed above the monthly production quota. Many of the workers I spoke to had been employed as garment workers in the Philippines' export processing zones, where they were paid piece-rates for exceeding quotas. The workers also expected to be fully compensated for overtime hours. As they note above, "We've noticed that we worked for a long hour of time. But why is it that some of our overtime not yet included in payroll." Workers described to me how they worked an average of five hours overtime in addition to their regular ten-hour work day (for a total of fifteen hours daily) for six days of each week in the month of April. In fact, there were even times when they were forced to work overnight as the factory management locked the doors to prevent them from returning to their dorms. Based on their calculations, the workers thought they would be paid an additional amount of B$243 ($133.68) on top of their monthly minimum wage of B$260 as well as any piece-rate pay when they received their wages in May.

Workers expressed concern that a portion of their wages was being affected by the fees automatically deducted from their monthly salaries to pay off loans to their Philippine-based recruitment agencies. As I have discussed elsewhere, Philippine labor recruiters generally pay for expenses related to migrants' employment overseas, like documentation fees (required by the various government agencies that comprise the migration bureaucracy), airfare, transportation to and from the airport, as well as fees for their services. These automatic deductions, workers complained, left them with as little as B$60 or about $33 a month. According to Eddie, "I went to Brunei with debts, I worked in Brunei with debts, and I left Brunei, still in debt."

In addition to being outraged because they were underpaid, many Philippine workers were also resentful that the Bangladeshis were

Figure 23. Inside factory compound in Brunei, 2001. Photograph by Melissa Alipalo.

being paid salaries equal to theirs. They believed that their Bangladeshi coworkers were less skilled, and they claimed that Philippine migrants were often given the task of training Bangladeshi workers. Filipina workers were convinced, therefore, that they deserved to be paid more. One worker complained, "It's very unfair that we train the Bangladeshis...but the wage increase was given only to Bangladeshis, not Filipinos. We're skilled and they aren't. We're more skilled than them. Why did the management do that? They insult the Filipino workers." This sentiment is also reflected in the workers' list of demands. If the Philippine state invests in the training of prospective migrants to make them more "competitive" in labor markets globally, we see how notions of skill are mobilized by Philippine migrants to make claims for higher wages though at the cost of ethnic solidarity on the shop floor.

The workers enlisted the aid of the Philippine government during the first round of the negotiations process, which included the workers themselves, the management, and representatives of the

Brunei labor department. As Josie explained, "One reason why we have embassies in different countries is because they are supposed to intercede for Filipinos, to meet with employers." The workers felt that the Philippine embassy could best represent their interests in Brunei, and, indeed, their Philippine-certified contracts state that they should turn to the Philippine embassy if all other negotiations with their employers fail.

During the second round of negotiations, however, workers learned that the Philippine embassy was barred from the meeting. Officials from Brunei indicated that according to Brunei law, the negotiations could only be tripartite, involving only the Brunei government, the workers, and management. The workers, however, insisted that all parties were already bound by the previous day's agreement to resume talks and that the Philippine embassy should be present to represent their interests.

The Philippine embassy, as well, believed that they had a right to be present at the negotiations because it was standard for them to participate in labor problems as their citizens' representatives. An embassy staff member was quoted in a Brunei newspaper as stating, "That is what we are here for, to look after the well-being of our nationals, and settle problems. The action to shut us off puzzles me." Registering a formal complaint at Brunei's Ministry of Foreign Affairs, the Philippine embassy was eventually allowed to resume its participation in the meetings. Philippine officials ended up standing in for the workers and negotiated directly with management, officials of the Brunei Labor Department, as well as officials of the Brunei Home Affairs Ministry (which oversees both the Labor Department and the Immigration Department), ostensibly on the workers' behalf.

Though all parties could agree that the workers' minimum monthly wage was in fact B$260, the management, supported by the Brunei government, contested the migrants' interpretations of piece-rate pay. Management contended that the piece-rate is applied to every *dozen* items produced over quota. Whereas Philippine migrants interpreted the piece-rate as applied to every single item they made in excess of the quota. Management insisted that the Brunei version of migrants' contracts and the provisions therewith must be applied. Workers were required to sign an employment contract upon arrival, which they assumed was identical to the contract they signed in the Philippines and which was certified by the POEA before they left. Though the contracts may have appeared the same, management argued, their interpretations were different, and it was the Brunei government's understanding of the provisions of the employment contract, not the Philippine government's, that should prevail. According to Boy, during the negotiations "the Brunei Labor [Department] said that any contract signed outside is invalid."

Rather than insisting on the validity of the workers' Philippine contract and the interpretations of its provisions, the Philippine government accepted the management's contentions and their offer to grant either a B$10 monthly increase for workers depending on their length of tenure with the company (B$10 for each year of their employment in the company up to B$20). The other option was an across the board raise of B$10 for all workers, regardless of length of employment, in other words, the maximum credit would be for only two years. The Philippine government accepted the terms of the management offer without even consulting the workers. Philippine officials later went about actively encouraging workers to accept the management offer and to determine which of the proposed wage increases they would accept. Even the vice president of the Philippines, visiting Brunei to officially prepare for the newly inducted Philippine president Arroyo's state visit, requested to meet with workers after several days of deadlock in a last attempt to convince workers to accept the management's proposal and return to work, stating, "Filipino workers should respect the local laws."[5] In the days following the vice president's meeting with workers, management officials and even representatives from the workers' Philippine-based recruitment agencies attempted to convince workers to accept the company's proposal and to return to work.

Eventually, half of the striking workers accepted the management's proposed salary increase and returned to work, while the other half requested to be removed from the premises of the factory and to return home, where they hoped to file claims through the Philippine government's grievance machinery.

The repatriation of those workers who intended to file claims in the Philippines, however, required the diplomatic intervention of the Philippine state. Having participated in the strike, the workers had violated Brunei law and should have been jailed. Philippine embassy staff, however, negotiated with the Brunei government to prevent the workers' jailing and to have the workers housed, alternatively, at Philippine government–owned sites (including the ambassador's residence and a workers welfare center run by the embassy) until travel arrangements could be made. According to the OWWA official based in Brunei:

> Under Brunei law, the employer should pay the flight tickets when the worker leaves, but, rather than have workers jailed, it was a concession on the part of the embassy to take responsibility for the tickets. It could have been a major problem diplomatically.

While the Philippine embassy in Brunei initially recommended that the employer be blacklisted by the Philippine Overseas Employment Administration (that is, blocked from being able to secure workers from the Philippines), it later issued an official acknowledgment of the employer's efforts at negotiating with the workers in good faith since they provided food and housing for the workers even when they stopped working. I learned in my interview with a representative at the DFA in the Philippines as well as an official at the Philippine-based headquarters of OWWA that the Philippine government had officially concluded that an amicable settlement had been reached.

Though diplomatic relations between Brunei and the Philippines were strained for the duration of the strike, they resumed normalcy almost immediately after the strike's resolution. The newly inaugurated president, Gloria Macapagal-Arroyo, made Brunei her first state visit. She hoped to leave Brunei with new possibilities for trade. The president even visited a garment factory employing Filipino migrants and addressed several thousand Filipinos at a public engagement during her stay. Not once during the visit was the issue of the strike raised in any significant way. It was as if it had not happened.

This case illustrates the limits and contradictions of the "rights" that the Philippine government extends to its overseas citizens through policies like RA8042. Filipino migrants, like those in Brunei, often draw on their home state for help and support and use the employment contract that their government has officially guaranteed as a means of asserting their labor rights in their countries of employment. Philippine officials intervene on workers' behalf, to some extent, as part of their mandate to "protect" their overseas citizens. Yet in the end, the Philippine government goes along with the demands of foreign employers and governments. In the Brunei case, not only did the Philippine government agree to the terms and conditions set by Malaynei's owners and the Brunei government; it actually assumed the role of convincing the workers to accept those terms and conditions. The Philippine state refused to assert the validity of the contracts it certifies, the very contracts that it heralds as the hallmark of migrants' "protection." It even spared employers a protracted labor dispute by repatriating those among the workers who continued to refuse to accept their offer. Finally, the Philippine state failed to sanction the employer for its bad labor practices. Despite contrary recommendations from some members of the embassy staff, the final position of the Philippine government was to affirm the employer's actions. In effect, the Philippine state participated in negotiating away the rights of Filipino workers. Though workers were protected from imprisonment as a consequence of "breaching" their contracts, the employers were absolved of all wrongdoing. In the end, the diplomatic relations between the two countries returned to normal, with the Philippine president making a state visit and securing key trade agreements only months after the labor dispute.

Struggling at Home

For the close to three hundred Filipino workers who were repatriated to the Philippines after the monthlong strike and negotiation process, the struggle was not over. Though they abandoned negotiations with their employers, the workers chose, upon recommendation from some Philippine embassy officials, to explore the grievance procedure available to migrants once they return to the Philippines through DOLE. As discussed earlier in this chapter, migrants can make claims against their employers for back or unpaid wages, as part of the set of "protective" measures of migrant citizenship. While workers who have returned to the Philippines are technically unable to file claims directly against their employers since they operate in foreign countries, they are able to file claims against the Philippine-based recruitment agencies that deployed them. Recruitment agencies are, by Philippine law, jointly liable with foreign employers. Workers are able to file claims directly against their recruitment agencies for charging them exorbitant placement fees. Monetary claims against employers are handled by the National Labor Relations Commission, which arbitrates between workers and recruitment agencies (who act as the local representatives of employers). Claims against recruitment agencies are addressed by the POEA.

Upon their return to the Philippines, the workers who participated in the strike in Brunei immediately set about filing monetary claims against their employers for back wages and overtime pay owed to them based on the same rationale they used in Brunei: that the employers had the responsibility of complying with the employment contract. They also filed claims against their recruitment agencies, charging that the agencies had engaged in illegal recruitment practices by deploying them to a problematic employer.

More than two months after their return to the Philippines, however, the workers' claims remained unresolved. They dealt with numerous challenges. First, workers found the claims-filing process confusing because they had to deal with two separate government agencies, each of which possessed its own procedures. Second, employers' and agencies' legal representatives were successful at convincing government arbitrators to process claims on an individual as opposed to a collective basis. According to one worker, "They're trying to divide us; we're losing our fire."

As I followed workers through the claims process, I observed how the POEA, in handling claims filed by workers against their employment agencies, had divided claims into "batches" of five to seven each, based on the specific agency responsible for deploying a particular group of workers. Apparently the factories in Brunei had secured workers from a number of different recruitment agencies in the Philippines. The agencies' attorneys offered different settlement amounts to each "batch" of workers. In one batch, I learned that workers were being offered P7,000 while another batch was offered P10,000. There did not appear to be any logic determining settlement amounts as some who had only recently been deployed to work in Brunei were offered more than those who had been working for a longer period. This settlement process served to weaken workers' unity and caused tensions among them.

In some cases, workers even found themselves the respondents to counterclaims made by their agencies. Agencies accused the workers of violating the terms of their contracts and sought to have the workers "watch-listed" and prevented from future overseas deployment. A counterclaim filed by one of the deploying recruitment agencies states:

> Complainants maliciously and capriciously filed the instant complaint against respondent agency despite having been assisted/helped in their overseas employment opportunity; to hide or cover their abuse or conceal their stubborn thrust to embarrass respondent agency and to destroy the goodwill earned by respondent agency with Principal/Employer as shown by way of STRIKE and to PRETERMINATE their signed contracts of employment, contrary to the terms and conditions of their contract with Principal/Employer for a term of two (2) years.... For their undisciplined acts, same OFWs who are complainants in the instant case ... are subject of DISCIPLINARY ACTION.

State arbitrators seemed to be positioned against the workers and were quite hostile. One arbitrator I observed seemed to be accusing a worker of lying on her claim form. The workers' response was, "We're the victim here; we're not lying. It's like you don't care." The arbitrator responded, "I'm saying just settle the problem. We can help you to settle, in a settlement no one wins, no one loses, everyone just gets along. It should be like that."

Suggesting that workers settle on the terms set by the recruitment agencies so "everyone just gets along" while taking an almost hostile stance toward workers indicates that the Philippine state is positioned less to advocate for workers and more to defend the interests of agencies and employers.

The state played a major role in ensuring that migrants would use the grievance system. Government officials preempted the possibility of workers engaging in more radical confrontations with employers' and agencies' representatives (and ultimately the Philippine government itself) as they did in Brunei. The state encouraged workers to consult with what were really state-sanctioned NGOs to help them with the grievance process. Immediately upon arrival in the Philippines, government officials carefully led workers through the airport terminal to avoid the press and activists from Migrante International. Migrante International, which played a key role in the Flor Contemplacion protests, had sent activists to the airport to meet the workers and help them continue their struggle now transplanted to the Philippines. Activists had been closely monitoring the strike and negotiations process as it was widely reported in the Philippine media. The Philippine government, however, permitted only migrants' family members access to the workers at the airport. The only outsiders with whom they allowed workers to interact were representatives of the OFW Family Club, an NGO that promised to secure the services of an attorney who had been endorsed by a member of the Philippine Senate.

Most workers were initially optimistic that their affiliation with the OFW Family Club would yield positive results, as it was rumored that a former NLRC head was a board member of the organization. They were optimistic too that the attorney assigned to them would be competent because he had been officially endorsed by a government official. Early in the grievance process, workers trusted that government officials and their networks would see to it that their claims would be granted. Yet after initially filing claims on workers' behalf at both the NLRC and the POEA, the attorney failed to show up at arbitration meetings. At the conclusion of my field research in August 2001 (two months after the strike) and after subsequent communication with workers in early September, the workers' claims had still not been settled. Some workers preferred Migrante's more confrontational style of engaging the Philippine government over the state's official grievance machinery, but they were only a small minority.

The Philippine government was veritably a "labor broker" in this struggle. On the one hand it supplied workers to the employer to begin with, and on the other hand it "brokered" settlements with both the employer and the Brunei government that were beneficial to all parties except for the workers.

Transnational Regulations

Not long after the final resolution of the strike was negotiated, Philippine president Gloria Macapagal-Arroyo arrived in Brunei. I had the opportunity to observe the newly inaugurated president's address to several thousand Filipino migrant workers. It became clear that her visit was not merely a routine state visit, but also an effort to smooth over relations with the Philippine migrant community, which had rallied to support the striking workers. At the same time, government officials used the public address to subtly reprimand migrants for their unruliness as workers in a foreign country. Though it has become routine for Philippine presidents to include a meeting with overseas Filipino workers whenever they go on official state visits abroad as a means of constituting migrants as a national community, this visit was timed to address the recent labor struggle.

I learned from migrants active in various organizations that a good portion of the president's itinerary included meetings with workers. In addition to a major public address, Arroyo was scheduled to mingle with selected representatives of Filipino groups at a special dinner party. Her itinerary included a tour of a garment factory, though, of course, not the factories where the strike took place.

There was clearly a great deal of excitement among Filipino migrants in Brunei about the president's visit. In fact, the sultan of Brunei had declared the day an official holiday for Philippine migrants so that they could attend the public address. The program at the theater was not supposed to start until 5:00 p.m., yet at 1:00 in the afternoon a line of Filipinos was wrapped around the theater anxious to get inside to secure one of the theater's three thousand seats (I was advised to go to the theater early if I wanted a seat myself). In the theater lobby workers would find themselves in yet another winding queue before being able to get into the theater proper. The mood was both formal and festive. Ushers, all volunteers from local Filipino organizations, were dressed in a traditional Philippine formal wear. While waiting in line I chatted with an older Filipino man who worked as a janitor at the sultan's palace. He proudly told me that he was one of the few who enjoyed the privilege of being invited to dinner with the president, her entourage, and embassy officials. By the time I was able to enter the theater (and I was supposed to be one of the early ones!) it was almost filled to capacity, and there were still many more people waiting to enter.

The Philippine embassy, anticipating the crowds, organized entertainment to fill the hours before the president's arrival. The entertainment program included several dance groups comprised of Filipino migrants based in Brunei and the winner of a locally organized karaoke contest. The highlight of the entertainment portion of the event was a comedienne brought in from Manila. Her risqué act, laden with sexual innuendo, was especially titillating to audience members because it was performed in the presence of Bruneian reporters and theater staff who were clearly Muslim. People laughed and pointed to the Bruneians in their midst whenever she cracked a sex joke. During her act, the comedienne called on embassy officials to participate. They all played along. The crowd went wild with laughter as government officials, including the administrator of the OWWA from Manila as well as the local OWWA representative, became the objects of the comedienne's jokes.

After her act, a radio personality–turned-congressman addressed the crowd. He went through an inventory of the various government services available to migrant workers through the embassy as well as in the Philippines. The highlight of his short speech, however, was a joke about a man who had the misfortune of being hit by bird droppings, "The man didn't complain. He thanked God. He didn't get mad but looked for a church and thanked God for not making *carabaos* [waterbuffaloes] fly." The entire theater erupted with laughter. He continued:

> The moral of the story is that you shouldn't forget to count your blessings. There may be a delay in your paycheck and people needing money you can't send; you'll have to return to the Philippines because your contract ends, but you still need to count your blessings that you're alive. People always approach me with problems, but I say don't forget your blessings. You should pray, "Thank you God. Even though thousands of Filipinos don't have jobs, I do. I'm here in Brunei."

The migrants clapped enthusiastically in response. The workers sat patiently through a repeat of the comedy act, which had to run a second time because the president was running late.

When she finally arrived, everyone in the theater stood up to catch a glance of the diminutive new president and attempted to squeeze in closer to the center aisle or to crowd the front of the stage to take her picture. An entourage of Philippine officials including the Philippine ambassador stationed in Brunei, the labor secretary, the secretary of defense, the secretary of the Department of Trade and Investment, the undersecretary of foreign affairs, the administrator of the OWWA, several Philippine senators, and her husband followed her up to the stage. I could hear the people around me try excitedly to identify the people she was with. As they stood, people cheered, "Ate Glo." "Ate" in Tagalog is a term of respect for elder sisters and had been popularized by her supporters since her inauguration to make her seem more accessible to ordinary people. Her presidency was under siege just the month before as supporters of former President Estrada rioted in the streets of Manila in what many dubbed "People Power 3" to protest his imprisonment on charges of graft and corruption. Estrada had been popularly represented as the president of the poor, in sharp contrast to Macapagal-Arroyo, who is the daughter of a former president. Despite the recent controversies surrounding her presidency, migrants in Brunei greeted her with enthusiasm.

Before her speech, the president presided over the inauguration of the newly elected officers of the Filipino Association and the Filipino Muslim Association based in Brunei. At the conclusion of the inauguration a representative of the migrant community addressed the president:

It's important that you visited us in the first year of your term. We know you care about us.... You can trust you have our whole-hearted support. When you were head of the Department of Social Welfare and Development, we got together to support the victims of the Mayon eruption with food and clothes. Now we pledge to support the presidential fund for OFWs. We've gotten together to support it. We're putting our money together to help start it.

He then handed her an envelope containing money. This is clearly an example of how migrants respond to calls to remit and reinvest in the Philippines.

A certain kind of social distance is bridged in these events as the state organizes social activities for workers, in this case a comedienne, to entertain them during what is an official visit. Moreover, high-ranking officials allow themselves to join in the events, playing along with the performances. The Philippine head of state herself participates in the inauguration of the Filipino migrant organizations' officers. Those same representatives, as well as the janitor whom I met, were special invitees to a party held at the president's hotel. Migrants get access to the highest elected officials in a way that is impossible for most Philippine citizens. Allowing overseas workers access, however limited, to the most powerful people in the "homeland," access only the very elite in the Philippines would ever have, is a means by which the state constitutes migrants as a distinct and privileged sector of society.

Migrants in turn see themselves as having a unique responsibility to their country of birth and, consequently, to the state. Hence, as in the case of migrants in Brunei, and throughout the world, they see it as their duty to contribute their efforts and earnings to aid those less fortunate among their *kababayan* (countrymen, which in Tagalog is gender-neutral), for instance by generating funds for victims of natural disasters or donating money to support state initiatives for OFWs.

Even if most migrants do not participate in migrant organizations, what is significant is that the Philippine embassy plays a key role in constituting overseas workers as a community. The work of the embassy is not limited to organizing major public engagements for the head of state. Part of the embassy's mission to migrant work-ers is to organize social activities, what one official called "cultural missions," like celebrations of the Philippines' Independence Day in June or other holiday events. These activities provide workers with the, sometimes rare, chance to get together with fellow *kababayan*. The state facilitates community formation among migrant workers, fostering their sense of being Filipino.

Based on my interviews of workers in Brunei active in these organi-zations, it was clear that migrants in specific groups had very close relationships with embassy officials. In fact, it was a former officer of a Filipino organization who took me to meet embassy staff in Brunei whom he knew on a first-name basis. Most Philippine embassies around the globe keep track of Filipino organizations, which become part of the government's official rosters. Migrants are therefore able to meet with elected officials whenever they are in the country.

After the awards ceremony, hours after migrants had first started gathering at the theater, the president launched into her speech. Most of her speech was spent commending workers for their role as the country's new national heroes:

> You've shown the world that one should be proud to be Filipino. You contribute to helping raise up our country. Because of you people finish school and homes are being built. . . . Because of your help, we're able to build small businesses. Because of your remittances, many barangays and cities and provinces have benefited from you. You have generated seven billion dollars in 2000 and eight billion dollars this year. This is the largest among other sectors. Hence, you are OFIs or "Overseas Filipino Investors." We need to change how we address you. You're more than workers; you're investors. Your investment is your productive years spent abroad. I salute you.

She gives the workers a military salute and people applaud.

The president further states, "We will continue to be heavily dependent on OFWs. Jobs in the Philippines are less than those abroad. It is your choice, but it is our humanitarian duty to strengthen your protection." Even as the president notes how the Philippines is "dependent on OFWs," she suggests that migrants who "choose" to migrate have thus performed an important duty for the state. The state here represents migration as a choice, as a means of naturalizing it, and therefore disavowing its role in exporting and thereby commodifying workers. This is a theme first expressed in the migration bureaucracy and repeated again in ritualized activities overseas. It is codified in migrant citizenship.

On a final note, President Arroyo says that not only are migrants important as investors to the Philippines, but as the nation's representatives abroad, they can play a role in bringing other foreign investors into the country:

> We trust that you can help to strengthen the relations between our two countries. I told the business community here that our best resources are our human resources. You are an attraction to investors to the Philippines. You can convince our friends in Brunei to come to our country.... OFWs are the immediate link to the Philippines.

This is perhaps what is most significant about state visits and other embassy-organized events for migrant workers. The purpose in constituting workers as a privileged sector of Philippine society, the purpose in constituting workers as part of a national community, is to maintain workers' sense of connection and obligation to the country they have left behind. The state not only constitutes migrants as part of the nation, but also endows them with a special role in Philippine society. Moreover, the state sets up initiatives, like the OFI program, that allow workers' to directly feed into the state's developmental initiatives.

Conclusion

The Philippine migrants' struggle in Brunei reflects some of the new complexities of work under contemporary conditions of globalization. In this case, Philippine migrants find themselves striking against factories (owned by Malaysians) established through subcontracting arrangements with major transnational corporations (U.S.-based Gap Inc.) in a foreign country (Brunei), where they are employed alongside migrants from other countries. The factories they are striking against, moreover, have entered into subcontracting arrangements with labor recruitment companies based in the Philippines who charge workers for having arranged their overseas employment. It is the Philippine state's diplomatic relations with countries like Brunei, however, that enables Brunei-based firms to secure labor from Philippine recruiters in the first place. Through bilateral labor agreements, Brunei, on the one hand, grants employment visas to Philippine workers. On the other hand, these agreements compel the Philippine government to adequately train and properly educate migrants about their responsibilities both as workers and as "guests" in Brunei. Meanwhile, workers press the Philippine government to intervene on their behalf. Given the provisions of the 1995 Overseas Filipinos and Migrant Workers' Act, the Philippine state is also required to act as a guarantor of migrants' employment contracts.

Struggles over the meaning of the employment contract demonstrate some of the inherent contradictions that underlie the Philippine state's role in the regulation of migration. Though the contract certification process is aimed at ensuring that Philippine migrants are protected from exploitation, in practice workers are forced to accept how employers and host governments interpret the terms of their employment. Philippine-certified documents are ultimately not legitimate in different national contexts. Migrant workers are unwittingly stripped of their protections once they leave the Philippines. The state's grievance process in the Philippines seems to work ultimately in recruitment agencies' and employers' favor as well.

Conclusion

The Globalization of the Labor Brokerage State

The central question that this book has explored is how and why citizens from the Philippines have come to be the most globalized workforce on the planet. I have argued that the answer to this question lies in the emergence of the Philippine state as a labor brokerage state. Though it is true that ordinary men and women in the Philippines desire employment abroad, and sometimes their desire to migrate may be motivated by completely noneconomic consideration, the task of *Migrants for Export* is to dissect the Philippine state's migration apparatus. As much as people make the final decisions about whether they will stay or whether they will leave, should they decide to migrate, the jobs and the places they imagine departing to are ultimately shaped by state actions. Moreover, my point in engaging in a critique of the state is to understand how state actions also impact the kinds of struggles migrants face when they are abroad. With the Philippines emerging as a so-called "model" of "migration management" it becomes important to situate its system of labor brokerage within the broader context of neoliberal globalization.

Building on the institutional antecedents of the U.S. colonial labor system, the postcolonial (or more precisely, the neocolonial) Philippine state erected a program of labor export to absorb spreading unemployment and underemployment and increasing rural displacement, the necessary consequences of neoliberal restructuring. Just as importantly, exporting labor became a profitable endeavor for the Philippine state as millions of U.S. dollars are generated from workers' remittances and even from the fees that the bureaucratic processing performed by the Philippine migration agencies requires.

Brokering labor is a strategy that economic and political elites in the Philippines have designed to deal with the dislocations of neoliberal globalization, dislocations it has had a strong hand in producing. Increasingly unemployed or underemployed, Philippine citizens simply cannot afford the rising cost of living. Services that were once publicly subsidized all come with a fee. The Philippines is in perennial economic and, consequently, political crisis. As the already small middle class tries to maintain its tenuous status, the precariousness of everyday life for the working classes and the poor compel many to join militant leftist movements, both legal and underground. The promotion of overseas employment is a means by which government leaders attempt to address the dislocations neoliberal globalization engenders. The state's promise of jobs to its citizens and, perhaps more importantly, the remittances migrants' send home, have helped the Philippines avert a major social catastrophe.

As a labor brokerage state the Philippine government mobilizes and then exports workers through a well developed and efficient migration bureaucracy. The Philippine government's ability to facilitate the out-migration of workers rests on its "authorizing" power. Though it has promoted the proliferation of private labor recruitment agencies as well as privately run training facilities to facilitate out-migration, the Philippine state nevertheless plays a decisive role in the globalization of workers. Few if any private labor recruiters can boast the global scope of the Philippine state apparatus. This apparatus, comprised of the Philippines' embassy and consular offices in scores of countries around the planet, identifies market trends for temporary contractual labor. These offices also initiate the process of negotiating diplomatic relations to formalize outflows of workers. These are not tasks that private recruitment agencies can accomplish.

The Philippine state has reconfigured ideas of national belonging to encourage its citizens to leave the Philippines while simultaneously fostering their ties to the homeland. Labor brokerage requires a particular set of relations between state and citizen, what I call migrant citizenship. The state represents migrants as "new national heroes," whose duty is to work overseas to support their loved ones and their home country through remittance earnings. Yet the state expects migrants "as heroes" to be exemplary representatives of the nation abroad by being law-abiding, diligent workers who return to the Philippines once their employment visas expire. Nationalism and citizenship have become the modalities through which the labor brokerage state mobilizes people to work as low-wage, temporary, gendered, and racialized laborers globally and secures their persistent relations to the nation-state.

Neoliberal globalization does not necessarily hollow developing states. Rather, these states have reconfigured notions of sovereignty, territoriality, and citizenship to produce citizen-workers primed to respond to the demands of global capitalism. Systems of labor brokerage may, in fact, be a necessary institutional form in this contemporary moment as a mode of organizing labor under conditions of neoliberal globalization. It offers a kind of "fix" for global capital and other neoliberalizing labor-importing states that demand temporary workers who will not make claims for membership and will return to their countries of origin once their jobs are done. On the one hand, neoliberal globalization is restructuring labor markets, organizing work, and thereby creating structural demands for foreign migrant workers. On the other hand, these demands are mitigated by nationalisms, themselves a product of neoliberalism and born out of the new kinds of insecurities citizens of different countries are made to feel in the face of precarious employment and dwindling social supports. Many are compelled to safeguard whatever limited entitlements their citizenship may offer under neoliberal conditions and call for immigration restrictions that limit the entry of foreigners and their ability to settle down. All of these economic and political factors create structural demands for temporary short-term migrant labor around the world, which labor brokerage states eagerly supply.

Philippine international migration is emblematic of globalization. In describing the increasing mobility of labor, it is often Filipina and Filipino migrants that scholars refer to as a primary example of this phenomenon. To suggest that the Philippine state is crucial to an understanding of Philippine international migration, as I do here, therefore, is to make an important intervention in the scholarship on international migration. Much of the scholarship on international migration of late has tended to reify capital flows from "above" to understand global labor flows or, in opposition to this scholarship, has examined globalization, specifically immigrant transnationalism from "below."[1] My research shows that the state plays a central role in both these processes, but just as importantly my research shows how the state links and mediates between these two processes through a case study of Philippine migration. I argue that the state is fundamental to globalization, just as importantly global processes constitute the state.

Though the Philippines has a distinct colonial and neocolonial history that accounts in large part for its development as a labor brokerage state, its is becoming more and more evident that the brokerage of labor is a highly portable and mobile strategy that different labor-sending states are adapting to their own ends within the changing context of globalization.

To study the Philippines is not merely to study a unique national case. To understand the Philippines' engagement in the brokerage of labor is to come to a better understanding of the processes and consequences of neoliberal globalization. A case study of the Philippine state's role in international migration as a labor brokerage state can offer important insights into understanding future trends in international migration under contemporary conditions of neoliberal globalization since it is a case where the labor-sending state's role in migration is most fully and clearly elaborated. There is much research demonstrating that migrant-sending states play a significantly vital role in building linkages with their (sometimes former) citizens overseas. States are motivated to create and sustain ties with their nationals abroad (citizen or not) to ensure that they remit or invest their incomes back "home." To regulate migrants' remittances states are creating new governmental bureaus to try to funnel migrants' earnings and direct them into the state's developmental initiatives.[2] They construct (new) nationalist discourses or even reform citizenship laws to (re)incorporate migrants.[3] The framework I lay out for explicating labor brokerage (that is, looking at the mobilization, export, and regulation of migrants) can be used as a framework for examining emergent forms of labor brokerage in other developing countries and determining to what extent labor brokerage is indeed a globalizing phenomenon. Further studies along these lines can contribute to broader debates about whether we are in fact apprehending "foundational realignments inside the state."[4]

The Philippine State and the Transnationalization of Labor Brokering

There is evidence that the Philippines is actually playing a role in transnationalizing labor brokerage as an institutional form. Labor brokerage has become a source of nationalist pride in the Philippines, one that officials attempt to export. One official claims:

> The Philippines is a lead model, according to the ILO, in migration management.... In one particular ILO convention, it was proposed that a central body be set up for all migrant-sending countries with [the Philippine] government to be a key player.... The Philippines is always invited to teach others attempting to develop their own labor export policies including Vietnam, Indonesia, Bangladesh, Sri Lanka, and Pakistan.

In another interview an official at ILAS stated that "the Philippines plays host to a number of foreign delegations including Vietnam, Indonesia, Thailand, and China. A former POEA administrator was even a consultant to Indonesia's labor ministry for a year." Philippine migration officials and bureaucrats have increasingly become experts in the global field of "migration management," working as consultants to other labor-sending countries or playing host to delegations from other countries because of the Philippines' highly developed migration bureaucracy. Yet another bureaucrat commented,

> The POEA has matured as an organization. Hence officials from other countries like Vietnam come here to learn how the Philippines has done [migration management]. Thailand, for instance, looks up to the Philippines in regard to its ability to manage migration even though it has surpassed the Philippines economically. This is also true of Indonesia. Officials from these countries come to the Philippines to learn about the system with Indonesia even requesting a memorandum of agreement that will ensure that there be an exchange of information in this area.

What this suggests is that it is in its expertise in "migration management," or what I call labor brokerage, that the Philippines is attempting to carve out a unique and legitimized role for itself in the neoliberal global order.

Discussions taking place in various multilateral settings provide evidence that the brokerage of labor is a constitutive feature of contemporary global processes. The idea of "Human Resources Development," or HRD, is now seen as critical to national as well as regional development among Asia Pacific Economic Cooperation (APEC) economies. Specifically, the idea of "Human Resource Development" refers not only to the training and skills development of the citizens of specific countries, but also to the mobility of labor throughout the regional economic bloc.

While there is recognition in multilateral forums like APEC that labor mobility is important to regional development, other kinds of multilateral venues, like ASEAN and WTO, have also begun to discuss the liberalization of trade in services, which will have consequences for labor migrants. Though multilateral organizations like ASEAN, APEC, and WTO concern themselves primarily with the liberalization of trade in goods, the liberalization of services has consequences for the movement of people as labor migration forms part of the trade in services. Both ASEAN and WTO are slated to begin new discussions on the trade in services, which may ultimately translate into greater mobility of labor both regionally and globally.[5]

The Philippine state is part of various multilateral organizations like APEC, ASEAN, and WTO, where it plays an important role in highlighting issues of migration and labor mobility. Its active participation in APEC discussions on migration when it hosted the APEC meetings of 1995, indicates that as a labor-sending state it is aggressively trying to liberalize labor mobility. Increased mobility across the region and around the globe means increased labor exports. Not only did President Ramos take important steps toward making the Philippines a presence in various international venues like APEC. It was in these forums that he attempted to make migration an issue to be given the kind of priority trade discussions are given in these venues.

He introduced the idea that migrants should be seen as "Internationally Shared Human Resources." Today, the Philippine state has become a key player in the U.N.-initiated Global Forum on Migration and Development (GFMD). In October 2008 it hosted a GFMD meeting where it shared its experiences of "migration management" with the international community.[6]

Multilateralism in the area of labor migration suggests that states recognize that state-to-state relations are a strategy by which to further the aim of making labor more mobile and flexible. Important to note too is the degree to which developing, labor-sending states like the Philippines play a key role in global processes through their efforts at liberalizing the mobility of labor in these multilateral forums.

As labor brokerage becomes a global "norm," the task of critiquing systems of labor brokerage, particularly that of the Philippines, becomes all the more urgent. As this study has shown, systems of labor brokerage favor employers and states more than they do ordinary people. However, collective transnational efforts of groups like Migrante International demonstrate how migrant workers are offering up novel conceptualizations of national and global belonging that undermine the project of the labor brokerage state as well as the hegemony of neoliberal globalization.

(Trans)nationalisms against the State

In July 2004, a little over a year after President Gloria Macapagal-Arroyo, in front of an audience of U.S. businesspeople in Washington D.C., pledged to facilitate the deployment of Philippine contractual workers to Iraq to take advantage of the job opportunities opened up by the U.S. occupation, Filipino migrant Angelo de la Cruz was kidnapped and threatened with beheading by Islamic extremists. His captivity triggered protests by Filipinos globally, led by Migrante International. As in the protests against the hanging of Flor Contemplacion, Migrante International mobilized member organizations of its transnational network to stage protests outside Philippine embassies and consular offices around the world as well as outside

Figure 24. Rally protesting ASEAN in Cebu City, Philippines, 2006. Photograph by the author.

of key government offices in the Philippines to pressure the Philippine government to intervene on de la Cruz's behalf. According to Migrante activists, de la Cruz's suffering was a direct consequence of the Philippine state's labor export program as well as its complicity with U.S. imperialism. Resolution of the crisis, therefore, could be achieved only with the Philippine state's termination of Philippine labor export to Iraq as well as the pulling out of its small contingent of troops engaged in the Iraqi front of the U.S. "war on terror." Despite the lucrative labor markets opened up by the U.S. occupation of Iraq, anticipated by the Philippine government only a year earlier, and its close alliance with the United States as part of the "coalition of the willing," the protests forced the Philippine state to comply with protesters' demands.

Migrant workers, as noncitizens, are often unable to assert their labor rights as rights more generally continue to be moored to formal membership or citizenship in a nation-state. The struggle of Filipina garment workers employed in Brunei starkly illustrates the limits of migrants' rights. In Brunei, migrants have no right to strike for better wages and working conditions. Even as some host states may extend rights to migrant workers, they are often only partial. Moreover, migrants may not always be able to assert international human rights norms in the way some scholars have anticipated.[7] At the same time, already beleaguered labor and other social movements in migrants' host countries may not have the capacity or the interest to fight for migrant workers' rights.

Filipino migrants' transnational political mobilizations on behalf of Angelo de la Cruz, Flor Contemplacion, and others since then illustrate how engagement with the Philippine state has become a vital means by which Philippine migrants have come to assert their rights both in their countries of employment as well as in the Philippines. It was Migrante International's grassroots transnational mobilizations in the wake of the Flor Contemplacion hanging that were instrumental in compelling the Philippine state to introduce RA8042, which in turn led to significant reforms in Philippine migration policy. Among the key elements of RA8042 is that it extends protections to migrants while they work abroad. RA8042 requires the Philippine government to intervene on their overseas citizens' behalf should their rights be violated in their countries of employment. The extent to which rights and entitlements supposedly guaranteed in RA8042 are actually granted to migrants, especially when they demand them as in Brunei, is questionable. Nevertheless, MI's capacity to effectively mobilize migrants to contest the state's neoliberal approach to migration is impressive.

Unlike their Brunei-based counterparts who used grievance mechanisms provided by the Philippine state through RA8042 to make wage and employment claims, those involved in Migrante International have been better able to engage the Philippine state by participating in actions outside of prescribed mechanisms and doing so transnationally. For instance, Migrante International member organizations have been successful in their wage and employment struggles not by enlisting Philippine state representatives to mediate

in wage and employment disputes, but by rallying in front of Philippine embassies and consular offices in their countries of employment
and demanding that the state advocate on their behalf on terms
defined by the migrants themselves. Migrants dealing with wage and
employment struggles in one country can rely on Migrante's affiliated organizations based in the Philippines and around the world
to hold solidarity actions in front of Philippine government offices
to press the state to address their issues. Scholars recognize that
the labor-sending state's intervention on behalf of its overseas citizens transnationally can be an important strategy for ensuring that
migrants' rights are protected. Labor-sending states, however, rarely
intervene because they either do not have the power or do not have
the interest.[8] Successful mobilizations by Migrante International suggest that when a labor-sending state is pressured transnationally by
its citizens, it is forced to intervene, and migrants' issues can be
successfully addressed.[9]

I suggest that with the absence of rights extended by migrants' host
states and without recourse to international human rights discourses,
Filipinos have turned to their home state to issue rights claims. In
some cases, Filipino migrants have called on the Philippine state to
intervene extraterritorially in labor disputes and human rights abuses.
In other cases, Filipino migrants through their embassies and consular
offices demand that the state provide them with additional services
as an extension of their rights and privileges as Philippine citizens
abroad. Beyond that, migrants attempt to weigh in on national
politics through absentee voting or direct action at Philippine government offices overseas. This citizenship is not conferred by states or
international institutions. In other words it is not "top down"; rather
the assertions of transnational citizenship have come from the "bottom up." Moreover, Philippine migrants have built a transnational
movement that originates in the homeland and extends out to the
diaspora.

Beyond struggling transnationally to enlist the Philippine state's
intervention on their behalf in wage and employment issues overseas, Migrante organizations based in the Philippines also spearhead
struggles for migration policy reform in the Philippines that ultimately

impact migrants' employment conditions overseas, and they mobilize their overseas affiliates to participate in these struggles. What makes Migrante unique is that it is a network that spans the globe and links together Philippine migrant groups around the world with groups of migrant workers' family members in the Philippines.

Migrants' engagement in transnational struggles also builds their capacity to engage effectively with labor movements and other civil society actors in their countries of employment to struggle for reforms in host countries that offer migrant workers rights and protections.

Through their engagement in the Migrante International network Filipina migrants, who are key leaders in building the network, bring domestic work (and other home-based care-related work) into the public sphere. They thereby denormalize domestic work as an extension of women's innate other-orientation, which foreign employers use to exploit and abuse them. Migrante International struggles to construct domestic work as a legitimate form of employment and that employers' homes ought to be subject to state labor regulations rather than an intimate space to be protected from external intervention.

Against more nationalist, paternalistic (and maternalistic) Philippine middle-class activists who campaign for employment bans on domestic work because it is "shameful" or because they think women who choose to work as domestics exercise poor judgment, Migrante activists instead struggle to maintain women's dignity on the job. If Migrante calls for an end to migration, it is a call for the end of structural inequalities within and between states that effectively force people to migrate. It is full citizenship that Migrante women (and men) activists fight for. Indeed, it is a radical revisioning of citizenship based on a noncapitalist order.

The struggle on behalf of Angelo de la Cruz further illustrates that Migrante ultimately sees migrants' well-being as inextricably tied to homeland politics. From Migrante's perspective, de la Cruz's safety and well-being could be assured only with the reform of Philippine migration policy in relation to labor deployment to Iraq and just as importantly with dramatic changes in the Philippine government's military and diplomatic commitments to the United States. Hence, it has closely allied itself with militant social movements in the Philippines that offer support and solidarity to migrants' issues around the world. Unlike most case studies of migrants' political transnationalism, which highlight how migrants engage in either immigrant rights or in homeland politics, Migrante International is an example of how migrants also link immigrants' rights overseas (that is, work and employment rights and basic human rights while living and working abroad) with political struggles at home.

Through its networks within and outside of the Philippines, Migrante International mobilizes migrants' transnationally to engage and contest the Philippine state's neoliberalism. Migrante's trans-national political mobilizations can therefore also be described as a form of counter-hegemonic (trans)nationalism. It is "counter-hegemonic" in that Migrante's linkages to the homeland are not with traditional political parties or other state institutions, as scholars have found in case studies of other forms of migrant transnationalism, but instead with radical social movements. It is (trans)national because, while Migrante is engaged in transnational political action around migrants rights, it is less invested in migrants' political incorporation in their host societies than in social transformation in the homeland.

Because it links migration to broader processes of neoliberal globalization, Migrante has become active in the progressive and militant nationalist movement of the Philippines, as represented by BAYAN (Bagong Alyansang Makabayan, New Patriotic Alliance) and engaged in the electoral process to secure progressive political candidates and parties including its own party-list organization, the Migrante Sectoral Party.

BAYAN plays a critical role in contesting the pernicious effects of neoliberalism, including trade liberalization and privatization, and it shares Migrante International's analysis that the Philippine state's active export of migrant workers is yet another neoliberal strategy that serves the interests of global capitalism since the state is com-plicit in providing privatizing foreign states and a range of capitalist firms with cheap labor. Moreover, BAYAN has consistently mobilized against corruption in the government since the Marcos dictatorship.

When President Fidel Ramos succeeded Corazon Aquino, he was keen on fast-tracking neoliberal economic policies with his

"Philippines 2000" plan. Ramos's administration played host to the Asia Pacific Economic Cooperation (APEC) in 1996 as a means of showcasing the Philippine commitment to neoliberal economic reform. Among the dignitaries participating in the APEC meetings was then–U.S. president Bill Clinton. As I discussed earlier, APEC was also a venue for President Ramos to put forward initiatives to expand the export of Philippine labor in the region. Though only a year old, Migrante International, as part of BAYAN, was a key participant in the anti-APEC parallel mobilizations that took place in Manila.

Ramos was succeeded by Joseph Estrada in 1998. Together with BAYAN, Migrante became critically involved in deposing President Joseph Estrada through what was called "People Power 2" in 2001. President Estrada had been undergoing an impeachment trial in the Philippine Senate on corruption charges, but when pro-administration Senators refused to admit evidence that would have likely convicted the president, Philippine citizens surged onto the streets of Metro Manila, calling for the president's resignation. Migrants were called upon by the beleaguered administration to continue sending their remittances to the Philippines to help buoy up the economy. However, they frequently expressed their disgust with the president through radio and television shows that encouraged them to call, text, and e-mail their opinions about the administration.

Migrante affiliates rallied in front of Philippine embassies to register their protest. In addition, they encouraged migrants to stop sending their remittances through the president's cronies' banks. Organizations of migrants based in Hong Kong, Japan, Korea, United States, Canada, Australia, Saudi Arabia, and throughout Europe, including Migrante member organizations as well as others, joined in the campaign. They also called on their family members to join protest movements in the Philippines.

Soon after President Estrada was succeeded by Gloria Macapagal-Arroyo in early 2001, national elections took place in the Philippines. Again migrants figured centrally in Philippine politics. As the newly launched "party-list" system allowed for different sectoral parties to participate in the national elections, guaranteeing them seats in the Philippine Congress if they received votes from a specific number of the electorate, Migrante activists mobilized to support the election of "Bayan Muna," which successfully brought three longtime progressive activists to power: Crispin Beltran, the leader of the militant left labor movement KMU (May First Movement); Liza Maza, leader of GABRIELA, the alliance of progressive women's organizations; and Satur Ocampo, former consultant to the communist-led National Democratic Front. MI would later establish its own Migrante Sectoral Party. As evidenced in its political mobilizations, for Migrante social change in the Philippines can come about only through the building of a global migrant workers' movement linked to a broader left movement that envisions a national democratic future for the Philippines.

Migrante International is a transnational migrant movement with an influence that spans the globe, but perhaps more importantly it has critical influence in the homeland. Migrante's allied organizations include groups in the countries where Filipinos work, as well as groups in the Philippines whose members are not in fact migrants themselves, but migrants' relatives and children. Because the state plays a role in deploying migrants globally, it becomes an immediate target for workers, sometimes even more immediate than their employers or their host countries.

The homeland continues to be the repository for rights and entitlements for migrants who have virtually no rights in the countries where they work. If migrants' sense of connection to the homeland and eventual return is the means by which the state is able to sustain the profitability of migration since workers can be trusted to remit their earnings and to come home at the end of their contracts, it is also their mooring to the homeland that is a means by which migrants make demands for rights from the Philippine government. Among these rights, as illustrated in the campaigns discussed here, are the right to intervention by the Philippines' consular and embassy offices in wage struggles overseas and the right to Philippine migration policies that protect migrants' economic well-being.

Migrante, however, is finally engaged in a transnational counter-hegemonic nationalism. What links Migrante organizations globally is a shared analysis of the causes and consequences of migration that ultimately displaces Filipinos from their families and, therefore, a shared commitment to struggling against the Philippine state. The transnational linkages they form in building a migrant workers' move-ment in the face of dispersal and displacement is a remarkable example of workers' resistance to the insidiousness of neoliberal globalization. Through organizations like Migrante, Filipino migrants forge an alter-native space of nationalist belonging and collective identification, a transnational community that is simultaneously anchored to the nation-state, even as it is constituted outside of and against the nation-state.

Finally, Migrante is also making transnational linkages with migrant groups around the world to build a global migrants' movement against neoliberal globalization. Migrante affiliates globally identify allies in their respective countries of employment to unite around a common vision of social justice. In late 2006, the organizing committee of the International Migrants' Alliance was convened, and it organized a founding congress in June 2008. One of the first major campaigns launched was protest actions against the Global Forum on Migration and Development that the Philippine government hosted in October 2008. The story of migrants' global solidarity continues to unfold, but the experiences of Migrante suggest that when migrants' effec-tively bridge ethnic, racialized, gendered, and other divides, they can be more successful in wage and employment rights while abroad. As Irene Fernandez, an activist based in Malaysia who was impris-oned for her work with migrants, declared in her keynote address of the International Migrants Alliance, "[We are a] globally mobile world proletariat . . . consolidating our selves as one race, one world." Stripped of the labor protections that citizen-workers enjoy and sel-dom entitled to even the most basic human rights when they go abroad; possessing, moreover, nationalities and citizenships that offer no guarantees but rather are a basis for differential exploitation, the proletarian subjectivity that Fernandez describes is a real possibility. Transnational formations like the International Migrants Alliance are sites for emergent forms of class-based identities and subjectivi-ties even as they are sites through which they are being constructed. Workers of the world unite? Perhaps.

Acknowledgments

The beginnings of this book can be traced to Union City, California, my hometown, where it was perfectly normal for my brother, Reuben, and I to smell the aroma of *chicken adobo* and to hear animated conversations in Tagalog as we walked home from school. This experience growing up ultimately led to the core questions that this book addresses: how and why Philippine (im)migrants come to find themselves on nearly every continent on the planet. My family, particularly my parents, Ruben and Daisy Rodriguez, and my late grandmother, Remedios Rodriguez, deserve the most thanks for their support in direct and indirect ways for this book's completion. My father instilled in me a very early love of books, and my mother's passion for research was formative in my development as a scholar. I found myself carving out a path in life that she, under different circumstances, would have made her own; instead, she, like many others before and after her, thwarted her personal desires to pursue nursing. My parents' investment in a set of a Funk and Wagnall's encyclopedia is probably what led me down the path to a Ph.D. in sociology! Informal·Tagalog lessons from my *lola* and her memories of Manila helped me to negotiate through the city when I went to live there to do field research. The tireless work of my *tito* Dolpo as a low-wage immigrant worker inspired me to keep a concern for workers' struggles at the center of my analysis.

Many thanks are due my colleagues and friends from the University of California, Berkeley. Jennifer Chun deserves credit for keeping me focused through graduate school and beyond; she has been a dear friend and *kasama*, and without her I am not sure this book would have been possible. Patrisia Macias has been a great source of support after Berkeley. Hung Thai, Tamara Kay, Josh Page, Jeff

Sallaz, Chris Weltzel, and Melissa Wilde have all been good to me in many different ways over the years. My dissertation chair, Michael Burawoy, continues to guide and inspire me; his active involvement in the shaping and completion of my dissertation, from which this book emerged, is unmatched. All of my professors at Berkeley were instrumental in my intellectual formation. Thanks are due to Nancy Chodorow, Peter Evans, Gillian Hart, Aihwa Ong, Raka Ray, and Barrie Thorne.

I had the good fortune to make a new home in a wonderfully vibrant place, and I have had the opportunity to be part of a number of different communities on campus that helped me work through this book: the Department of Sociology, the Institute for Research on Women, the Department of Women and Gender Studies, the Collective for Asian American Studies, and the Immigration Group at the Eagleton Center for Politics. There are too many people at Rutgers to thank, but special appreciation goes to Ethel Brooks, Carlos Decena, Catherine Lee, Ann Mische, Pat Roos, Kristen Springer, Zaire Dinzey Flores, Allan Issac and Zakia Salime. Ann and Pat, my mentors in the sociology department, have been cheering me to the finish line with this book since day one here at Rutgers. Catherine, Kristen, and Zakia made my new life as a junior faculty member much more bearable, and I also thank the wonderful undergraduate and graduate students I have met along the way, particularly Manjusha Nair, Carlos, Zaire, Allan, and Ethel thanks for plotting and scheming with me and making academic life all that I have wanted it to be. Research for parts of this book was supported by the Rutgers' Research Council, Global Opportunities Award, and the Byrne Family First Year Seminars.

Beyond Rutgers I am blessed to have a great transnational network of friends and colleagues to depend on: Catherine Raissiguier, Helen Schwenken, Oscar Campomanes, Nerissa Balce, Peter Chua, Martin Manalansan, Rick Bonus, Emily Ignacio, Anna Guevarra, and Melissa Alipalo. I reserve a heartfelt *salamat* to Lucy Burns and R. Zamora Linmark, who have been constant and patient companions on this long journey. My fore"mothers" in Filipino studies (you know who you are) who span the Pacific paved the way for those of us who decided to take this road. And finally I am grateful to my *kasamas* throughout the world, especially my comrade/sister/friend/student, Valerie Francisco, who inspire me with their visions for and work toward a better future. *Makibaka huwag matakot!*

I thank Jason Weidemann at the University of Minnesota Press for his early interest and enthusiastic support for this project and John Eagleson for seeing it to its completion.

I owe a special debt of gratitude to my beautiful boys, David and Amado. Amado, you have brought me so much joy. If there is something that I can claim as my greatest achievement, it is certainly not this book, but you. Your sense of curiosity and fierce sense of justice (at such a young age!) are a wonder and a gift. David, you crossed many oceans to stand by my side. You have always been a source of strength for me as we faced challenges in our lives together, and your personal history of struggle and triumph has given me hope during times of despair. I love you both dearly.

Appendix

Mapping an Ethnography of the State

The beginnings of my field research can be traced to the end of a thirteen-hour flight from San Francisco to the Philippines that I took in the summer of 1997. As the plane prepared to land, flight attendants pushed carts of duty-free items through the aisles one final time. They sold makeup, alcohol, jewelry, and cigarettes. Other passengers and I quickly bought up the brand-named luxury goods to give as *pasalubong* (souvenir gifts) to relatives who anxiously awaited our arrival. Sometimes entire barrios make the trek to the Ninoy Aquino International Airport in Manila to greet arriving family members.

Once the duty-free cart had made its last round, the flight attendants distributed customs declaration cards. Everyone was required to fill them out and present them to immigration authorities once the plane landed. People paused to enumerate the *pasalubong* they were likely to have already packed in carefully weighed *balikbayan* (nation returnee) boxes. In addition to the duty-free luxury items purchased on the plane, *pasalubong* often includes everyday items like towels, toilet paper, clothing, and canned goods. Most, if not all, of the passengers, including me, had checked in one or more of these distinctive boxes; most, if not all, of the passengers on this flight were Filipino.

Along with a list of the contents of my *balikbayan* boxes, the form asked that I identify my citizenship. I was compelled to reflect on my family's migration history. My parents immigrated separately to the United States in the early 1970s. My mother, a nurse, was able to immigrate ahead of my father, who narrowly missed President Ferdinand Marcos's declaration of martial law in 1972. I was born in San Francisco not long after he arrived in the United States.

I found it difficult, however, to answer the seemingly simple set of questions. I am not technically a *balikbayan,* that is, one who has emigrated and is either an ex– or dual Filipino citizen; nor am I an OFW. Yet I am also not merely a tourist. I found myself not fitting into the official categories that the Philippine state designates for present and former Philippine nationals and yet uncomfortable about the options I have. I was forced to pull out my passport with "United States" emblazoned on its blue cover to note down my passport number on the customs form. I officially declared on the form that I am a U.S. citizen in the Philippines as a tourist for both pleasure and business — I would have the pleasure of reuniting with relatives I had not seen for a decade, and I would be conducting the business of sociological research.

Soon a hush overcame the passengers. Necks craned to peer eagerly out the windows. As the flickering lights of Manila welcomed us, I looked around me. These people whom I had barely noticed for the duration of the flight, people who were merely co-passengers, were suddenly transformed in my eyes as we collectively experienced the excitement of arrival. I recognize them now as *kababayans,* or fellow nationals. I felt a new sense of intimacy and connection with them. My heart jumped as I caught a glimpse of the Manila skyline. I was overcome with emotion as the plane touched the ground. I found myself weeping. I looked around, and I was not alone.

In those brief moments on the airplane, I found myself acutely aware of the ways in which I was constituted outside of the Philippine nation-state as I confronted state categories for citizens through the process of filling out a routine customs form. At the same time, however, I felt a sense of community with other people on the plane, a feeling that defies state categorizations. The feelings elicited by the customs form prompted me to ask how and to what extent mundane practices of state impact migrants' ideas of nationalism, citizenship, and belonging. In other words, what are some of the unintended consequences of bureaucratic practices, especially those of the state's migration bureaucracy? The state uses the customs form as a means of collecting tariffs. Yet it brought out in me different sets of responses, including exclusion, embarrassment, and disappointment. My sense of connection with fellow passengers in spite of state categorizations led me to ask how community and belonging are being imagined and practiced by (im)migrants in what has become a veritable labor diaspora. At the same time, the very presence of these various categories on the customs form merits its own analysis. Why has the state created these different categories for its overseas citizens? Of course, this then begs the question, Why are there so many Philippine citizens overseas to begin with?

My experiences on the airplane in 1997 ultimately prompted me to examine the Philippine state and migration in particular ways. *Migrants for Export* is based on qualitative research including ethnography, interviews, and archival research conducted mainly in the Metro Manila area of the Philippines. My field research took place over the course of ten years: four months in 1997, fourteen months in 2000–2001, six weeks in 2003, two weeks in 2006, and an additional two weeks in 2008.

What is unique about my work, however, is that I applied ethnographic methods to a study of the state. My field research included observation of the daily operations (as well as the more flamboyant public activities like Migrant Heroes Week) of the Philippine government's various migration agencies, including POEA, DFA, and OWWA. At the POEA I also observed a sampling of the mandatory training sessions that domestic workers and entertainers undergo: respectively the Pre-Departure Orientation Seminar (PDOS) and the Pre-Departure Showcase Preview (PDSP). I was also able to observe a handful of TESDA-certified training centers for domestic workers and entertainers and to interview six administrators of these programs. Finally, I also spent time at the Ninoy Aquino International Airport observing the departure and arrival processes as well as other grandiose activities, like the heroes' welcome, that took place there.

I supplemented my ethnographic research with in-depth interviews of nineteen state officials and bureaucrats both in the Philippines and Brunei. Interviewing methods are important to understanding state practices because they provide us with a perspective on how officials understand and actually do their work. Studying laws and policies alone is insufficient to grasping how state agents interpret and implement them. I had the good fortune of meeting some of the highest ranking officials in the migration bureaucracy as well as people who would be considered petty bureaucrats. In short, I interviewed those responsible for the state's migration policies and programs as well as those whose task it is to implement those policies and programs and who must deal with migrants on a daily basis. I managed to secure most of the interviews entirely on my own. Most of these government representatives were incredibly candid with me. I believe this was due, in part, to the fact that I generally refrained from tape recording interviews with them. Additionally, officials seemed to be very open with me because they were impressed and puzzled by the fact that I, as a Filipina American, had an interest in the "homeland," studied at a prestigious university, and could speak Tagalog! There was only one case that I tape-recorded an interview with an official, who was the highest-ranking official of the POEA. I was confident that taping this interview would not prevent this official from being open with me since the interview was secured through a contact who had a relative who was a close friend of the official. These interviews ranged in length from being as short as forty-five minutes to as lengthy as several hours.

Being able to gain state representatives' trust, I was given access to a wide array of internal government documents that have been important in shaping my understanding of the migration bureaucracy. I was also able to do archival research at the POEA library.

In the process of conducting ethnographic work at the Philippine government's migration agencies, I was able to meet workers who I spoke to informally and in some cases was able to formally interview at a later time. My relatives, friends, and colleagues proved to be a secondary source of interviews. While I was in the Philippines, for instance, the cousin I am closest to, Peter Magalit III, was in the process of preparing for a job in Saudi Arabia. Meanwhile, Peter's sister-in-law was in the process of trying to secure a factory job in Taiwan. They both left while I was still in the field. In all, I conducted formal interviews with seventy-three workers (thirty-seven of these workers were migrant activists, as I discuss below).

In addition to my ethnography of the state in the Philippines, I conducted a weeklong research trip to Brunei in 2001, where I tracked how the Philippine government intervened in the garment workers' strike that I describe in chapter 6. Before leaving for Brunei, I managed to interview Philippine officials at the DFA and OWWA who were monitoring the case. In Brunei, I meet with embassy officials who then connected me with the leaders of several Filipino migrant community groups. Fortuitously, I was able to introduce myself to those workers who decided to stay behind after the negotiations process at the grocery store right outside the factory in question. I met other Filipino workers at the hotel where I was staying who introduced me to yet other workers, including garment workers employed in other factories. They then helped to arrange for me a tour of one of the factories so I could get a better sense of working conditions.

With migration being such a normal part of everyday life in the Philippines, it was quite easy for me to meet returned or prospective migrants on a day-to-day basis. It seemed that nearly every time I took a taxi to the POEA or other migration offices was an occasion to discuss migration with the drivers. Invariably, they would either be returned migrants who had invested their earnings to purchase and operate the taxi or were migrant workers earning extra cash in between contracts. I learned to keep a small notebook handy in anticipation of these meetings and managed to keep copious notes of these exchanges, however brief. I was able to interview (formally and informally) fairly equal numbers of men and women mainly bound for work in Asian and Middle Eastern countries (they are, after all, the top importers of Filipino workers). According to my notes, I conducted twenty-seven informal interviews, but I am certain that I met many more migrants than are actually written about in my notebooks. My subjectivity as a Filipina and daughter of immigrants allowed

me incredible degrees of access to people. Moreover, feminist interviewing techniques informed my interview style. I was easily able to
establish a rapport with migrants who honestly and graciously shared
their fears and aspirations with me.

The bulk of my field research was conducted in 2000 and 2001.
During that time People Power 2 brought down President Joseph
Estrada on corruption charges. I was therefore able to track the
various ways the issue of migration was used by contending political rivals. Very often these rivalries would be reflected in the daily
operations of the bureaucracy.

I also worked as a participant-observer in the headquarters of
Migrante International in Manila. This gave me the opportunity both
to watch and to join in the daily activities, and in the process I
was able to secure interviews with a total of thirty-seven activists.
Moreover, I was able to get hold of their organizational material.
During a trip to the Philippines in 2006 and to Hong Kong in 2008,
I was able to observe two international conferences organized by
MI, where they brought together migrant activists from around the
world to share experiences and to plan internationally coordinated
activities.

Most if not all of the names I use in this book are pseudonyms.
Moreover, I generally refer to the various Philippine migration
officials as that: migration officials. I may also use the term "bureaucrat" or "government representative." Apart from identifying which
migration agency they work for or the specific department within
each agency they work with, and on a few occasions signaling their
rank in the agency if they occupy a high office, I have refrained
from identifying them by name. The fact is, most of the officials I
interviewed were mid-level bureaucrats with titles like "Director" or
"Officer in Charge." What is striking is that regardless of gender or
tenure of employment in whatever agency they worked for, they dis-
played a remarkable consistency in the ways they spoke about the
Philippines' migration policy. They aped official policy statements in
their use of terms like the importance of priming Filipino workers
to be globally "competitive," in disavowing that the state actually

exports workers, in emphasizing that they are ultimately in the business of giving Philippine citizens a chance to make well-informed choices about working abroad. What is important to this project, however, is that they were able to elaborate how these policies are ultimately implemented on the ground. They also provided me access to internal government documents that helped me to understand the backstage aspects of policy implementation, and they allowed me to see what migration programs looks like from the perspective of workers.

Notes

Introduction

1. For a discussion on the racialization of Filipinos under U.S. colonialism in the Philippines, see, for instance, Julian Go, "Racism and Colonialism: Meanings of Difference and Ruling Practices in America's Pacific Empire," *Qualitative Sociology* 27, no. 1 (2004). Rick Baldoz does an interesting analysis of how these racializing discourses then played out when Filipinos arrived on U.S. shores to work during the colonial period: Rick Baldoz, "Valorizing Racial Boundaries: Hegemony and Conflict in the Racialization of Filipino Migrant Labor in the United States," *Ethnic and Racial Studies* 27, no. 6 (2004).

2. See http://institution.ibon.org/ for Ibon publications.

3. According to Carlos, the Philippines is second only to Mexico as the largest exporter of workers in the world. See Ma. Reinaruth D. Carlos, "On the Determinants of International Migration in the Philippines: An Empirical Analysis," *International Migration Review* 36, no. 1 (2002). The 2005 figures from the International Organization for Migration (IOM), however, put the Philippines as third after China and India in terms of total migrant population. See for example, International Organization for Migration, *World Migration 2005: The Costs and Benefits of International Migration* (Geneva: International Organization for Migration, 2005).

4. For the most recent statistics on Philippine migration see www.poea .gov.ph/. The only stock estimate of Philippine migrants available from the POEA is from 2004. This figure is likely to be higher at present.

5. Ibid.

6. From www.census.gov.ph/.

7. See Wayne A. Cornelius et al., *Controlling Immigration: A Global Perspective*, 2d ed. (Stanford, Calif.: Stanford University Press, 2004). Their study provides a multicountry perspective on immigration control.

8. Numerous studies have been conducted exploring, among other issues, the myriad reasons why people (especially women) from the Philippines seek to live and work outside of the Philippines. The following are just a small sampling: Pauline Gardiner Barber, "Agency in Philippine Women's Labour Migration and

Provisional Diaspora," *Women's Studies International Forum* 23, no. 4 (2000); Kimberley A. Chang and Julian McAllister Groves, "Neither 'Saints' nor 'Prostitutes': Sexual Discourse in the Filipina Domestic Worker Community in Hong Kong," *Women's Studies International Forum* 23, no. 1 (2000); Nicole Constable, *Maid to Order in Hong Kong* (Ithaca, N.Y.: Cornell University Press, 1997); Rhacel Salazar Parreñas, *Servants of Globalization: Women, Migration, and Domestic Work* (Stanford, Calif.: Stanford University Press, 2001).

9. See POEA, "Middle East," www.poea.gov.ph/html/prospects2004/html.

10. Enrico Dela Cruz, "Philippines 2007 Overseas Workers' Remittances at Record 14.4 Billion Dollars," *Thomson Financial News Limited* (2008), www.forbes.com/markets/feeds/afx/2008/02/15/afx4659876.html. The IMF ranks the Philippines third after Mexico and India in terms of remittance earnings. See International Monetary Fund, *Migration and Foreign Remittances in the Philippines* (Washington, D.C.: International Monetary Fund, 2005).

11. See, for instance, Michael Burawoy, "The Functions and Reproduction of Migrant Labor: Comparative Material from Southern Africa and the United States," *American Journal of Sociology* 81, no. 5 (1976).

12. Neferti Tadiar, "Domestic Bodies of the Philippines," *Soujourn* 12, no. 2 (1997): 5.

13. Saskia Sassen, "Women's Burden: Counter-Geographies of Globalization and the Feminization of Survival," *Journal of International Affairs* 53, no. 2 (2000): 101.

14. I provide a detailed discussion of my methodological approach to studying labor brokerage in the Appendix.

15. To understand labor brokerage I pay attention to officials' and bureaucrats' interpretation and implementation of the government's migration policies and face-to-face interactions between low-level civil servants and citizens in the daily operations of the migration bureaucracy. By focusing on the more mundane aspects of state practice, I necessarily understand "the state" as a complex institution populated by a range of agents and characterized by numerous contradictions even as it may be oriented by broader rationalities or "interests."

16. David Harvey, *A Brief History of Neoliberalism* (Oxford: Oxford University Press, 2005), 65.

17. Aihwa Ong, *Neoliberalism as Exception: Mutations in Citizenship and Sovereignty* (Durham, N.C.: Duke University Press, 2006), 12.

18. See John Williamson, "What Washington Means by Policy Reform," in *Latin American Adjustment: How Much Has Happened,* ed. John Williams (Washington D.C.: Institute for International Economics, 1990) for an elaboration of the key precepts of the Washington Consensus.

19. William I. Robinson, "Beyond Nation-State Paradigms: Globalization, Sociology and the Challenge of Transnational Studies," *Sociological Forum* 13, no. 4 (1998): 173.

20. See the discussions in Revathi Krishnaswamy and John C. Hawley, eds., *The Postcolonial and the Global* (Minneapolis: University of Minnesota Press, 2008).

21. Here I am referring to "development" as it is understood within the framework of modernization theory. See the following for critiques of modernization and development that I am informed by Arun Agrawal, "Poststructuralist Approaches to Development: Some Critical Reflections," *Peace and Change* 21, no. 4 (1996); Peter Chua, Kum-Kum Bhavnani, and John Foran, "Women, Culture and Development: A New Paradigm for Development Studies," *Ethnic and Racial Studies* 23, no. 5 (2000); Arturo Escobar, *Encountering Development: The Making and Unmaking of the Third World* (Princeton, N.J.: Princeton University Press, 1995); Peter Evans, "Imperialism, Dependency, and Dependent Development," in *Dependent Development*, ed. Peter Evans (Princeton, N.J.: Princeton University Press, 1979); James Ferguson, *The Anti-Politics Machine: Development, Depoliticization, and Bureaucratic Power in Lesotho* (Minneapolis: University of Minnesota Press, 1994); William I. Robinson, "Transnational Processes, Development Studies, and Changing Social Hierarchies in the World System: A Central American Case Study," *Third World Quarterly* 22, no. 4 (2001).

22. Ligaya McGovern, "Labor Export in the Context of Globalization: The Experience of Filipino Domestic Workers in Rome," *International Sociology* 18, no. 3 (2003): 518.

23. E. San Juan, "Interrogating Transmigrancy, Remapping Diaspora: The Globalization of Laboring Filipinos/as," *Discourse* 23, no. 3 (2001): 69.

24. Ong, *Neoliberalism as Exception*, 14. See Graham Burchell, "Liberal Government and Techniques of the Self," in *Foucault and Political Reason: Liberalism, Neo-Liberalism and Rationalities of Government*, ed. Andrew Barry, Thomas Osborne, and Nikolas Rose (Chicago: University of Chicago Press, 1996), for a similar approach to understanding neoliberal governmentality. Of course, see Gordon Colin, "Governmental Rationality: An Introduction," in *The Foucault Effect: Studies in Governmentality*, ed. Graham Burchell, Colin Gordon, and Peter Miller (Chicago: University of Chicago Press, 1991), for Foucault's original explications of governmentality.

25. Studies documenting the deleterious impacts of the Washington Consensus are numerous. To cite just a few: Robinson, "Transnational Processes, Development Studies, and Changing Social Hierarchies in the World System." For an examination of the gendered consequences of development in Asia, see

Esther Ngan-ling Chow, ed. *Transforming Gender and Development in East Asia* (New York: Routledge, 2002).

26. Ligaya McGovern, "Neo-Liberal Globalization in the Philippines: Its Impact on Filipino Women and Their Forms of Resistance," *Journal of Developing Societies* 23, no. 15-35 (2007).

27. Overseas employment is not the Philippine state's only strategy for containing social unrest (as exemplified by the proliferation of radical social movements). As I discuss in chapter 1, it has always violently suppressed oppositional groups even under conditions of "democracy."

28. Clyde W. Barrow, "The Return of the State: Globalization, State Theory, and the New Imperialism," *New Political Science* 27, no. 2 (2005): 125.

29. Aihwa Ong, *Flexible Citizenship* (Durham, N.C.: Duke University Press, 1999); Aihwa Ong, *Neoliberalism as Exception: Mutations in Citizenship and Sovereignty.*

30. L. H. M. Ling, "Sex Machine: Global Hypermasculinity and Images of the Asian Woman in Modernity," *Positions: East Asia Cultures Critique* 7, no. 2 (1999): 285.

31. Howard Winant, *The New Politics of Race* (Minneapolis: University of Minnesota Press: 2004), ix.

32. Former Singaporean prime minister Lee Kwan Yu has been especially vocal in describing the Philippines as a failure. See Rob Vos and Josef T. Yap, *The Philippine Economy: East Asia's Stray Cat: Structure, Finance, and Adjustment* (New York: St. Martin's Press, 1996), for a characterization of the Philippines not as an "Asian Tiger," but as Asia's "stray cat."

33. "Entertainment" refers to women's employment, mainly in Japan's bars and restaurants, as singers, dancers, hostesses, and other related jobs.

34. Martin Ruhs and Philip Martin, "Numbers vs. Rights: Trade-Offs and Guest Worker Programs," *International Migration Review* 42, no. 1 (2008): 249–50.

35. Some scholars seem to share international organizations' "win-win-win" assessments of systems of temporary labor migration. See, for example, Jonas Widgren and Philip Martin, "Managing Migration: The Role of Economic Instruments," *International Migration* 40, no. 5 (2002). Also see Hein De Haas, "International Migration, Remittances and Development: Myths and Facts," *Third World Quarterly* 26, no. 8 (2005). These studies fail to critique the neo-liberal logic that underlies notions of remittance-driven "development" in the way that I do here.

36. This is a term Philippine state officials use to describe their labor export program. International organizations and some migration scholars use this term

to describe states' attempts at regulating temporary migration, or "guest worker" regimes.

37. See for instance, Nana Oishi's work, where she documents the labor-exporting policies of several countries in Asia: Nana Oishi, *Women in Motion: Globalization, State Policies and Labor Migration in Asia* (Stanford, Calif.: Stanford University Press, 2005). Susan Bibler Coutin's ethnography of the El Salvadorian state documents practices that are quite similar to those engaged in by the Philippine state: Susan Bibler Coutin, *Nations of Emigrants: Shifting Boundaries of Citizenship in El Salvador and the United States* (Ithaca, N.Y.: Cornell University Press, 2007).

38. For an elaboration on the role of labor recruitment agencies in facilitating out-migration from the Philippines, see Manolo I. Abella, "The Role of Recruiters in Labor Migration," in *International Migration Prospects and Policies in a Global Market*, ed. Douglas S. Massey and J. Edward Taylor (Oxford: Oxford University Press, 2004); James A. Tyner, "The Gendering of Philippine International Labor Migration," *Professional Geographer* 48, no. 4 (1996). James Tyner also examines the role of private recruiters, with close attention to the ways they shape gendered migration: Tyner, "The Gendering of Philippine International Labor Migration"; J. A. Tyner, "Asian Labor Recruitment and the World Wide Web," *Professional Geographer* 50, no. 3 (1998); J. A. Tyner, "The Web-Based Recruitment of Female Foreign Domestic Workers in Asia," *Singapore Journal of Tropical Geography* 20, no. 2 (1999).

39. John Torpey, "Coming and Going: On the State Monopolization on the 'Means of Legitimate Movement,'" *Sociological Theory* 16, no. 3 (1998).

40. Edward S. Cohen, "Globalization and the Boundaries of the State: A Framework for Analyzing the Changing Practice of Sovereignty," *Governance: An International Journal of Policy and Administration* 14, no. 1 (2001): 79.

41. Saskia Sassen, "Regulating Immigration in a Global Age: A New Policy Landscape," *Parallax* 11, no. 1 (2005): 38.

42. William I. Robinson, "Social Theory and Globalization: The Rise of a Transnational State," *Theory and Society* 30 (2001): 172.

43. Here I am informed by ethnographic approaches to studying the state like Begonia Aretxaga, "Maddening States," *Annual Review of Anthropology* 32 (2003): 383–410; Thomas Blom Hansen and Finn Stepputat, "Introduction: States of Imagination," in *States of Imagination*, ed. Thomas Blom Hansen and Finn Stepputat (Durham, N.C.: Duke University Press, 2001), 1–38. James Ferguson and Akhil Gupta, "Spatializing States: Toward an Ethnography of Neoliberal Governmentality," *American Ethnologist* 29, no. 4 (2002): 981–1002.

1. The Emergence of Labor Brokerage

1. *Jeepneys* are surplus World War II U.S. military vehicles that have been converted into a mode of public transportation.

2. See James A. Tyner, "Global Cities and Circuits of Global Labor: The Case of Manila, Philippines," *Professional Geographer* 52, no. 1 (2000).

3. This chapter focuses mainly on the Philippine–U.S. colonial labor system. For studies of Filipino migration under the Spanish see, for example, Tyner, "Global Cities and Circuits of Global Labor"; Lorraine J. Crouchett, *Filipinos in California: From the Days of the Galleons to the Present* (El Cerrito, Calif.: Downe Place Publishers, 1982).

4. See Paul Kramer, *The Blood of Government: Race, Empire, the United States, and the Philippines* (Chapel Hill: University of North Carolina Press, 2006).

5. Luzviminda Francisco, "The First Vietnam: The U.S.-Philippine War of 1898," *Bulletin of Concerned Asian Scholars* 5 (1973).

6. See Paul Kramer, "The Water Cure: Debating Torture and Counter-insurgency — A Century Ago," *New Yorker*, February 25, 2008.

7. Yen Le Espiritu, *Filipino American Lives* (Philadelphia: Temple University Press, 1995).

8. See for a discussion of elites' role in the colonial state: Julian Go, *American Empire and the Politics of Meaning* (Durham, N.C.: Duke University Press, 2008).

9. Suchen Chan, *Asian Americans: An Interpretive History* (Boston: Twayne, 1991).

10. Espiritu, *Filipino American Lives*, 5.

11. Dorothy B. Fujita-Rony, *American Workers, Colonial Power: Philippine Seattle and the Transpacific West, 1919–1941* (Berkeley: University of California Press, 2003).

12. Linda Maram, *Creating Masculinity in Los Angeles's Little Manila: Working-Class Filipinos and Popular Culture, 1920s–1950s* (New York: Columbia University Press, 2006).

13. Benjamin V. Carino, "The Philippines and Southeast Asia: Historical Roots and Contemporary Linkages," in *Pacific Bridges: The New Immigration from Asia and the Pacific Islands*, ed. James T. Fawcett and Benjamin V. Carino (Staten Island, N.Y.: Center for Migration Studies, 1987).

14. See his excerpted piece in Daniel B. Schirmer and Stephen Rosskamm Shalom, eds., *The Philippines Reader: A History of Colonialism, Neocolonialism, Dictatorship and Resistance* (Boston: South End Press, 1987).

15. Barbara Posadas and Roland L. Guyotte, "Unintentional Immigrants: Chicago's Filipino Foreign Students Become Settlers, 1900–1941," *Journal of American Ethnic History* 9, no. 2 (1990).

16. Lt. Donald F. Duff and Cdr. Ransom J. Arthur, "Between Two Worlds: Filipinos in the U.S. Navy," *American Journal of Psychiatry* 123, no. 7 (1967).

17. Catherine Ceniza Choy, *Empire of Care* (Durham, N.C.: Duke University Press, 2003).

18. Ibid., 65.

19. Ibid.

20. Choy discusses St. Luke's Medical Center in her book. Some historical background on the hospital is available on-line at www.stluke.co.ph.

21. See Brett H. Melendy, "The Filipino Exclusion Movement 1927–1935" (Quezon City, Philippines: Institute of Asian Studies, 1967), John B. Christiansen, "The Split Labor Market Theory and Filipino Exclusion: 1927–1934," *Phylon* 40, no. 1 (1979).

22. Espiritu, *Filipino American Lives*; Yen Le Espiritu, "Filipino Navy Stewards and Filipina Health Care Professionals: Immigration, Work, and Family Relations," *Asian and Pacific Migration Journal* 11, no. 1 (2002).

23. Joaquin Gonzalez, *Philippine Labour Migration: Critical Dimensions of Public Policy* (Singapore: Institute of Southeast Asian Studies, 1998), 119.

24. William J. Pomeroy, *An American Made Tragedy: Neo-Colonialism and Dictatorship in the Philippines* (New York: International Publishers, 1974).

25. Daniel B. Schirmer and Stephen Rosskamm Shalom. *The Philippines Reader: A History of Colonialism, Neocolonialism, Dictatorship, and Resistance* (Boston: South End Press, 1987), 89.

26. Pomeroy, *An American Made Tragedy.*

27. Ibid.

28. Stephen R. Shalom, *The United States and the Philippines: A Study of Neocolonialism* (Philadelphia: Institute for the Study of Human Issues, 1981), 73.

29. Gary Hawes, *The Philippine State and the Marcos Regime* (Ithaca, N.Y.: Cornell University Press, 1987).

30. Ibid.

31. Walden Bello and Robin Broad, "The International Monetary Fund in the Philippines," in *The Philippines Reader: A History of Colonialism, Neocolonialism, Dictatorship, and Resistance,* ed. Daniel B. Schirmer and Stephen Rosskamm Shalom (Boston: South End Press, 1987).

32. See Maruja M. B. Asis, "The Overseas Employment Program Policy," in *Philippine Labor Migration: Impact and Policy,* ed. Graziano Battistella and Anthony Paganoni (Quezon City, Philippines: Scalabrini Migration Center, 1992); Graziano Battistella, "Philippine Migration Policy: Dilemmas of a Crisis," *Sojourn: Journal of Social Issues in SE Asia* 14, no. 1 (1999).

33. John Williamson, "What Washington Means by Policy Reform," in *Latin American Adjustment: How Much Has Happened,* ed. John Williams (Washington, D.C.: Institute for International Economics, 1990).

34. For a critical analysis of tourism policies in Asia see Linda Richter, *Politics of Tourism in Asia* (Honolulu: University of Hawaii Press, 1989).

35. Cynthia Enloe, *Bananas, Beaches, and Bases* (Berkeley: University of California Press, 1989).

36. Samir Amin, *Capitalism in the Age of Globalization* (New York: Zed Books, 1998).

37. Saskia Sassen provides a now-classic explication of how export-oriented manufacturing employment can induce international migration. Saskia Sassen, *The Mobility of Labor and Capital: A Study in International Investment and Labor Flow* (New York: Cambridge University Press, 1988).

38. David Wurfel, *Filipino Politics: Development and Decay* (Ithaca, N.Y.: Cornell University Press, 1988).

39. Eva-Lotta E. Hedman and John T. Sidel, *Philippine Politics and Society in the Twentieth Century* (New York and London: Routledge, 2000), 29.

40. Ben Reid, "The Philippine Democratic Uprising and the Contradictions of Neoliberalism: Edsa Ii," *Third World Quarterly* 22, no. 5 (2001): 779.

41. Ben Reid, "Poverty Alleviation and Participatory Development in the Philippines," *Journal of Contemporary Asia* 35, no. 1 (2005): 34.

42. Eduardo T. Gonzalez, "Equity and Exclusion: The Impact of Liberalization on Labor," in *The State and the Market: Essays on a Socially Oriented Philippine Economy,* ed. Filomeno S. Santa Ana (Quezon City: Ateneo de Manila University Press, 1998).

43. Bulletin, "DOLE Says Program for OFWs Top Priority," *Manila Bulletin,* June 21, 2000.

44. See Ibon Foundation, Inc., *Stop the Killings in the Philippines* (Quezon City, Philippines, 2007) or www.ibon.org/.

45. DOLE, "Labor Day Supplement 159–2001" (2001).

2. A Global Enterprise of Labor

1. Pei-Chia Lan, *Global Cinderellas: Migrant Domestics and Newly Rich Employers in Taiwan* (Durham, N.C.: Duke University Press, 2006), 53.

2. Eric Neumayer, "Unequal Access to Foreign Spaces: How States Use Visa Restrictions to Regulate Mobility in a Globalized World," *Transactions of the Institute of British Geographers* 31 (2006): 73.

3. Pierre Bourdieu, "Rethinking the State: Genesis and Structure of the Bureaucratic Field," in *State/Culture: State Formation after the Cultural Turn,* ed. George Steinmetz (Ithaca, N.Y.: Cornell University Press, 1999), 67.

4. Hilary Cunningham and Josiah McC. Heyman, "Introduction: Mobilities and Enclosures at Borders," *Identities: Global Studies in Culture and Power* 11, no. 3 (2004): 293.

5. Horng-Luen Wang, "Regulating Transnational Flows of People: An Institutional Analysis of Passports and Visas as a Regime of Mobility," *Identities: Global Studies in Culture and Power* 11 (2004): 359.

6. See www.poea.gov.ph/.

7. www.gov.im/isleofman/facts.xml.

8. David Harvey, *Condition of Post-Modernity* (Cambridge, Mass.: Blackwell Publishers, 1989).

9. See Geraldine Pratt, *Working Feminism* (Philadelphia: Temple University Press, 2004).

10. Rochelle Ball, "Divergent Development, Racialised Rights: Globalised Labour Markets and the Trade of Nurses — the Case of the Philippines," *Women's Studies International Forum* 27, no. 2 (2004): 129.

11. The "domestic" employers TESDA trains workers for, of course, are multinational or transnational corporations.

12. See Joseph Berger, "Filipino Nurses, Healers in Trouble," *New York Times,* January 27, 2008.

13. See www.tesda.gov.ph/.

14. Christopher L. Erickson et al., "From Core to Periphery? Recent Developments in Employment Relations in the Philippines," *Industrial Relations* 42, no. 3 (2003). Not only is English the medium of instruction; it continues to be the language of government and commerce. For a history of public education in the Philippines, see Chester L. Hunt and Thomas R. McHale, "Education and Philippine Economic Development," *Comparative Education Review* 9, no. 1 (1965).

15. See www.tesda.gov.ph/.

16. Nicola Piper, "Gendering the Politics of Migration," *International Migration Review* 40, no. 1 (2006).

17. Kimberley A. Chang and L. H. M. Ling, "Globalization and Its Intimate Other: Filipina Domestic Workers in Hong Kong," in *Gender and Global Restructuring: Sightings, Sites and Resistances,* ed. Marianne H. Marchang and Anne Sisson Runyun (New York: Routledge, 2000), 28.

18. Bridget Anderson, *Doing the Dirty Work? The Global Politics of Domestic Labour* (New York: Zed Books, 2000), 2.

19. Nicole Constable, *Maid to Order in Hong Kong* (Ithaca, N.Y.: Cornell University Press, 1997).

20. "Japayuki" is a term, often considered derogatory, used to refer to women working as entertainers in Japan.

21. Anna Romina Guevarra, *Marketing Dreams, Manufacturing Heroes: The Transnational Labor Brokering of Filipino Workers* (New Brunswick, N.J.: Rutgers University Press, 2009), 4. My own research confirms her findings.

22. POEA, *2007 Annual Report* (Mandaluyong City, Philippines: POEA, 2007).

23. *POEA Rules and Regulations* (Mandaluyong City, Philippines: POEA, 1991).

24. See, for example, Vivek Chibber, "Bureaucratic Rationality and the Developmental State," *American Journal of Sociology* 107, no. 4 (2002); Peter Evans, *Embedded Autonomy: States and Industrial Transformation* (Princeton, N.J.: Princeton University Press, 1995).

25. Maruja M. B. Asis, "The Overseas Employment Program Policy," in *Philippine Labor Migration: Impact and Policy,* ed. Graziano Battistella and Anthony Paganoni (Quezon City, Philippines: Scalabrini Migration Center, 1992), 79.

26. Lan, *Global Cinderellas,* 56–57.

27. Based on my inquiries at the South Korean embassy in the Philippines.

28. See Ecumenical Institute for Labor Education and Research (EILER), "Labor Flexibilization and Imperialist Crisis: Intensifying Exploitation, Dismantling Job Security, Liquidating Unions," *Institute of Political Economy Journals* no. 26 (2000).

29. TNT, or "tago ng tago" (hide and hide), refers to undocumented migration.

30. Aristide Zolberg, "The Next Waves: Migration Theory for a Changing World," *International Migration Review* 23, no. 3 (1989): 406.

31. See Melissa Wright, *Disposable Women and Other Myths of Global Capitalism* (New York: Routledge Press, 2006), 29.

3. Able Minds, Able Hands

1. POEA, "Filipino Workers: Moving the World Today" (Mandaluyong City, Philippines, POEA).

2. Claire Kim's argument about the racial triangulation of Asians in the U.S. context informs my thinking here (see Claire Jean Kim, "The Racial Triangulation of Asian Americans," *Politics and Society* 27, no. 1 [1999]). However, scholars looking at emergent racialized orders in the NICs of Asia are also important here. See Pei-Chia Lan, *Global Cinderellas: Migrant Domestics and Newly Rich Employers in Taiwan* (Durham, N.C.: Duke University Press, 2006).

3. Claire Kim and Taeku Lee make the following observation: "How do racial hierarchies originate and reproduce? In the post-1965 era, no single myth has done more work in this regard than the model-minority myth, which holds that Asian Americans are hardworking, law-abiding, thrifty, family-oriented, education-revering people who have made it in American society and should serve as a 'model.'" See Claire Kim and Taeku Lee, "Interracial Politics: Asian Americans and Other Communities of Color," *PS: Political Science and Politics* 34, no. 3 (2001): 634. And, as Jasbir Puar and Amit Rai remind us, the "model minority" myth is centered on the heterosexual Asian family. See "The Remaking of a Model Minority: Perverse Projectiles under the Specter of (Counter)Terrorism," *Social Text-80* 22, no. 3 (2004): 75–104.

4. C. T. Mohanty, "Women Workers and Capitalist Scripts: Ideologies of Domination, Common Interests, and the Politics of Solidarity," in *Feminist Genealogies, Colonial Legacies, Democratic Futures,* ed. J. M. Alexander and C. T. Mohanty (New York: Routledge, 1997). See other studies about the gender and racial politics of production like Aihwa Ong, *Spirits of Resistance and Capitalist Discipline: Factory Women in Malaysia* (Albany: State University Press of New York, 1987), or Kathryn Ward, *Women Workers and Global Restructuring,* ed. Kathryn Ward (Ithaca, N.Y.: Cornell University Press, 1990).

5. Juanita Elias, "Stitching-up the Labour Market: Recruitment, Gender, and Ethnicity in the Multinational Firm," *International Feminist Journal of Politics* 7, no. 1 (2005): 99.

6. See Melissa Wright, *Disposable Women and Other Myths of Global Capitalism* (New York: Routledge Press, 2006).

7. Gary Gereffi, "Rethinking Development Theory: Insights from East Asia and Latin America," *Sociological Forum* 4, no. 4 (1989).

8. Philippine Overseas Employment Administration, "International Labor Market Update 2007" (Mandaluyong City, Philippines: POEA, 2007).

9. Refer back to my discussion of U.S. colonialism in the Philippines in chapter 1.

10. See Helen Sampson, "Transnational Drifters or Hyperspace Dwellers: An Exploration of the Lives of Filipino Seafarers Aboard and Ashore," *Ethnic and Racial Studies* 26, no. 2 (2003): 253–77.

11. See www.poea.gov.ph/. The POEA publishes its market information on a regular basis.

12. Mehmet Odekon, "Globalization and Labor," *Rethinking Marxism* 18, no. 3 (2006): 422.

13. See, for example, Stephen Castles and Mark J. Miller, *The Age of Migration* (New York: Guilford Press, 2003); Timothy C. Lim, "Racing from the Bottom

in South Korea: The Nexus between Civil Society and Transnational Migrants," *Asian Survey* 43, no. 3 (2003): 423–42; and Jon Goss and Bruce Lindquist, "Placing Movers: An Overview of the Asian-Pacific Migration System," *Contemporary Pacific* 12, no. 2 (2000): 385–414.

14. I discuss these national anxieties in more depth in chapter 5.

15. See Robyn Rodriguez, "The Labor Brokerage State and the Globalization of Filipina Care Workers," *Signs* 33, no. 4 (2008).

16. POEA, "Hong Kong," www.poea.gov.ph/html/prospects2004/html.

17. Julie Javellana-Santos, "Manila Launches New Program to Train 'Supermaids,'" *Arab News,* August 4, 2006.

18. Nana Oishi, *Women in Motion: Globalization, State Policies, and Labor Migration in Asia* (Stanford, Calif.: Stanford University Press, 2005).

19. POEA, "International Labor Market Update 2007."

20. POEA, *2007 Annual Report* (Mandaluyong City, Philippines: POEA, 2007).

21. Nicole Constable, *Maid to Order in Hong Kong* (Ithaca, N.Y.: Cornell University Press, 1997); Geraldine Pratt, "From Registered Nurse to Registered Nanny: Discursive Geographies of Filipina Domestic Workers in Vancouver, B.C.," *Economic Geography* 75, no. 3 (1999). For discussions of the colonial representations of the Filipina and their implications for today, see Nerissa S. Balce, "The Filipina's Breast: Savagery, Docility, and the Erotics of American Empire," *Social Text* 24, no. 287 (2006). Also see Vernadette Gonzalez and Robyn Rodriguez, "Filipina.Com: Filipina Bodies on the Cyberfrontier," in *Asian America.Net,* ed. Rachel Lee and Sau-Ling Wong (New York: Routledge, 2003) for a discussion on the circulation of representations of Filipinas on the Internet and its relationship to the globalization of Filipina workers.

22. Ethel Brooks, *Unraveling the Garment Industry: Transnational Organizing and Women's Work* (Minneapolis: University of Minnesota Press, 2007), 97.

23. See Pei-Chia Lan, " 'They Have More Money but I Speak Better English!' Transnational Encounters between Filipina Domestics and Taiwanese Employers," *Identities* 10 (2003); for a discussion of how the ability to speak English becomes a means by which Filipina domestic workers try to assert their status.

24. Oishi, *Women in Motion.*

25. Philippine Overseas Employment Administration, "Existing Bilateral Labor and Similar Agreements" (Mandaluyong City, Philippines: POEA, 1999).

26. Ibid.

27. See Oishi, *Women in Motion,* 50. She attributes Filipina entertainers' migration to Malaysia and Japan to bilateralism between the Philippines and each of those two countries.

28. For the full report see www.poea.gov.ph/.

29. Philippine Overseas Employment Administration, "Rise in Deployment of Professional and Technical Workers Boosts Remittances" (Mandaluyong City: POEA, 2007).

30. POEA, *2003 Annual Report* (Mandaluyong City: POEA, 2003).

31. Panda Ragnhild and Smita M. Lund, "The Asian Financial Crisis: Women's Work and Forced Migration," *Norsk Geografisk Tidsskrift* [Norwegian Journal of Geography] 54, no. 3 (2000): 128–33.

32. Philippine embassy in Israel, "RP Asks Israel to Go Slow on Deportation of Migrants," www.polota.com/news3.htm; Philippine Overseas Employment Administration, "Deployment of Workers to Israel" (Mandaluyong City, Philippines: POEA, 1999).

33. For a discussion on undocumented migration in Israel, see Lan, "'They Have More Money but I Speak Better English!'"; Adriana Kemp, "Labour Migration and Racialisation: Labour Market Mechanisms and Labour Migration Control Policies in Israel," *Social Identities* 10, no. 2 (2004).

4. New National Heroes

1. Investments in nationalism and citizenship appear to be important to labor-sending states beyond the Philippines too. Scholars of immigration and transnationalism, for instance, have documented how labor-sending states in Latin America have introduced a number of policies aimed at extending political rights such as dual citizenship or the right to vote overseas to "reinforce emigrants' sense of enduring membership." See Peggy Levitt and Rafael de la Dehesa, "Transnational Migration and the Redefinition of the State: Variations and Explanations," *Ethnic and Racial Studies* 26, no. 4 (2003). The States' purpose in reinforcing this sense of membership may be related to specific state actors' political aims in the homeland or it may be aimed at attempting to draw on immigrants to exert political influence in their host countries. Often, however, states reinforce emigrants' political ties to the homeland as a means of securing their remittances and investments.

2. Kathleen Weekley, "Nation and Identity at the Centennial of Philippine Independence," *Asian Studies Review* 23, no. 3 (1999): 338.

3. See, for example, Will Kymlicka, "Multicultural Citizenship," in *The Citizenship Debates*, ed. Gershon Shafir (Minneapolis: University of Minnesota Press, 1998); Christian Joppke, "How Immigration Is Changing Citizenship: A Comparative View," *Ethnic and Racial Studies* 22, no. 4 (1999); Ruud Koopmans, *Contested Citizenship: Immigration and Cultural Diversity in Europe* (Minnesota: University of Minnesota Press, 2005).

4. David Fitzgerald, *A Nation of Emigrants: How Mexico Manages Its Migration* (Berkeley: University of California Press, 2009), 4.

5. Cristina Blanc, "Balikbayan: A Filipino Extension of the National Imaginary and of State Boundaries," *Philippine Sociological Review* 44, nos. 1–4 (1996). Also see L. Basch, N. Schiller, and C. Blanc, *Nations Unbound: Transnational Projects, Postcolonial Predicaments, and Deterritorialized Nation-States* (London: Gordon and Breach, 1994).

6. These discourses continue to plague the Philippines and have been especially vociferous with respect to nurses. In my interview a practicing dentist who was training to be a caregiver in order to qualify for a U.S. visa described how people in her class, including the instructor, tried to discourage her from leaving the country. "Don't leave; just use your skills here," was their admonishment.

7. Vicente Rafael, " 'Your Grief Is Our Gossip': Overseas Filipinos and Other Spectral Presences," *Public Culture* 9 (1997). Robyn Rodriguez, "Migrant Heroes: Nationalism, Citizenship and the Politics of Filipino Migrant Labor," *Citizenship Studies* 6, no. 3 (2002).

8. "Code of Discipline" (Mandaluyong City, Philippines: POEA, 1991).

9. Filomeno V. Aguilar Jr., "The Dialectics of Transnational Shame and National Identity," *Philippine Sociological Review* 44, no. 1–4 (1996): 11.

10. Reynaldo Ileto, *Pasyon and Revolution: Popular Movements in the Philippines, 1840–1910* (Quezon City, Philippines: Ateneo de Manila University Press, 1979).

11. Felicisimo O. Joson, "Memorandum Circular No. 46, Series of 1996" (Mandaluyong City, Philippines, 1996).

12. POEA, "Information Primer for Filipino Seafarers" (Mandaluyong City, Philippines: Manpower Development Division, POEA, 1997).

13. Welfare Services Branch, "Request for Assistance Letter" (Mandaluyong City, Philippines: POEA, 2000?).

14. Martin IV Manalansan, "Queer Intersections: Sexuality and Gender in Migration Studies," *International Migration Review* 40, no. 1 (2006): 226.

15. Kathleen Weekley, "Nation and Identity at the Centennial of Philippine Independence," in *Asian Studies Review* 23, no. 3 (1999): 341.

16. Rob Wilson, "Imagining 'Asia-Pacific': Forgetting Politics and Colonialism in the Magical Waters of the Pacific. An Americanist Critique," *Cultural Studies* 14, no. 3/4 (2000): 568.

17. Commission on Filipinos Overseas, *Handbook for Filipinos Overseas*, 5th ed. (Manila: Department of Foreign Affairs, 2000).

18. Ibid.

5. The Philippine Domestic

1. Elsewhere I discuss Migrante International's role in the protests and their articulations of nationalism and citizenship that radically depart from those favored by the state. See Robyn Rodriguez, "Migrant Heroes: Nationalism, Citizenship, and the Politics of Filipino Migrant Labor," *Citizenship Studies* 6, no. 3 (2002): 341–56. I look at Migrante International's transnational organizing efforts beyond the Philippines and the specific role of Filipina migrants in "Challenging the Limits of the Law," in *Globalization and Third World Women: Exploitation, Coping and Resistance,* ed. Ligaya McGovern and Isidor Wallimann (Hampshire, U.K.: Ashgate Press, 2009): 49–63.

2. Ruby Palma Beltran and Gloria F. Rodriguez, eds., *Filipino Women Migrant Workers: At the Crossroads and Beyond Beijing* (Quezon City, Philippines: Giraffe Books, 1996).

3. I discuss the brokerage of care workers in "The Labor Brokerage State and the Globalization of Filipina Care Workers," *Signs: Journal of Women and Culture in Society* 33, no. 4 (2008): 794–99.

4. Neferti Tadiar, "Domestic Bodies of the Philippines," *Sojourn: Journal of Social Issues in Southeast Asia* 12, no. 2 (1997): 169.

5. Nira Yuval-Davis, "Gender and Nation," *Ethnic and Racial Studies* 16, no. 4 (1993): 628.

6. Neferti Xina M. Tadiar, *Fantasy-Production: Sexual Economies and Other Philippine Consequences for the New World Order* (Hong Kong: Hong Kong University Press, 2004).

7. I am informed in part by work like that of Graham Burchell, "Liberal Government and Techniques of the Self," in *Foucault and Political Reason: Liberalism, Neo-liberalism, and Rationalities of Government,* ed. Andrew Barry, Thomas Osborne, and Nikolas Rose (Chicago: University of Chicago Press, 1996), 19–36.

8. See Anna Romina Guevarra, "Managing 'Vulnerabilities' and 'Empowering' Migrant Filipina Workers: The Philippines' Overseas Employment Program," *Social Identities* 12, no. 5 (2006): 537. Nana Oishi discusses the gender politics of migration policy in the Philippines as well as in other Asian countries in *Women in Motion: Globalization, State Policies, and Labor Migration in Asia* (Stanford, Calif.: Stanford University Press, 2005). James Tyner offers a good analysis of the constructions of entertainers in James A. Tyner, "Constructions of Filipina Migrant Entertainers," *Gender, Place, and Culture* 3, no. 1 (1996).

9. See Helen Schwenken and Pia Eberhardt, "Gender Knowledge in Economic Migration Theories and in Migration Practices," GARNET Working Paper

no. 58/08 (2008) available at www.garnet-eu.org/fileadmin/documents/working_papers/5808.pdf/.

10. Ibid., 3.

11. Sylvia Chant and Cathy McIlwaine, *Women of a Lesser Cost: Female Labour, Foreign Exchange, and Philippine Development* (Quezon City, Philippines: Ateneo de Manila University Press, 1996).

12. For an incisive critique of the media's discussions of the violence suffered by migrant women see "Domestic Bodies," chapter 3 in Neferti Tadiar's *Fantasy Production*.

13. Michael Duenas, "The Maricris Sioson Story: A Dance with Death," *Philippine Free Press*, November 2, 1991; "The Maricris Sioson Case: Filipina's Death in Japan Remains 'Unresolved.' Government Asked to Investigate Another Filipina Dancer's Death in Fukushima," *Philippines Free Press*, November 2, 1991.

14. Sandra Harding, ed., *Feminism and Methodology* (Bloomington: Indiana University Press, 1987).

15. Ma. Alcestis Abrera-Mangahas, "Public Attitudes towards Female Overseas Workers: Implications for Philippine Migration Policy" (Quezon City, Philippines: Social Weather Stations, 1994), 18.

16. Eviota Uy, *The Political Economy of Gender: Women and the Sexual Division of Labor in the Philippines* (London: Zed Books, 1992).

17. Abrera-Mangahas, "Public Attitudes towards Female Overseas Workers," 18.

18. Anne McClintock, "Family Feuds: Gender, Nationalism and the Family," *Feminist Review* 44, no. 1 (1993): 63.

19. Sarah A. Radcliffe, "Gendered Nations: Nostalgia, Development, and Territory in Ecuador," *Gender, Place and Culture* 3, no. 1 (1996): 6.

20. DOLE, *White Paper on Overseas Employment*, 52. Department of Labor and Employment, Republic of the Philippines, 1995.

21. Ibid.

22. Neferti Tadiar, "Domestic Bodies of the Philippines," *Sojourn: Journal of Social Issues in Southeast Asia* 12, no. 2 (1997): 169.

23. Wendy Brown, "Finding the Man in the State," in *The Anthropology of the State: A Reader*, ed. Aradhama Sharma and Akhil Gupta (Malden, Mass.: Blackwell Publishing, 2006), 189.

24. Barbara Cruikshank, "Revolutions Within: Self-Government and Self-Esteem," in *Foucault and Political Reason: Liberalism, Neo-Liberalism and Rationalities of Government*, ed. Andrew Barry, Thomas Osborne, and Nikolas Rose (Chicago: University of Chicago Press, 1996), 235.

25. In the end, any kind of nonreproductive sex is prohibited. Indeed, so is reproductive sex. Migrant women are ultimately discouraged from marrying and having children with locals in the countries where they work.

26. Anna Romina Guevarra, "Managing 'Vulnerabilities' and 'Empowering' Migrant Filipina Workers: The Philippines' Overseas Employment Program," *Social Identities* 12, no. 5 (2006): 525.

6. Migrant Workers' Rights?

1. Aihwa Ong, *Flexible Citizenship* (Durham, N.C.: Duke University Press, 1999): 215.

2. POEA, *Migrant Workers and Overseas Filipinos Act of 1995* (Mandaluyong City, Philippines: POEA, 1996).

3. See www.poea.gov.ph/.

4. Malanei is a pseudonym.

5. Nikko Fabian, "Visiting Philippine President Wants Countrymen in Brunei to Behave," *BruneiDirect.com*, 2001.

Conclusion

1. Work by world systems scholars like Saskia Sassen might be characterized as scholarship that looks at capital flows "above" the state to understand international migration. Lately, the scholarship has been particularly attentive to immigrants' transnational practices "below" the state. A plethora of research has been done in this vein. The following is hardly an exhaustive list of publications. Alejandro Portes provides a review of the scholarship in "Conclusion: Theoretical Convergences and Empirical Evidence in the Study of Immigrant Transnationalism," *International Migration Review* 37, no. 3 (2003): 874–92. For a comparative U.S.–European review of the field see Alejandro Portes and Josh DeWind, "A Cross-Atlantic Dialogue: The Progress of Research and Theory in the Study of International Migration," *International Migration Review* 38, no. 3 (2004): 828–51. A sampling of the scholarship on Latino/Caribbean immigrants' transnationalism in the United States includes Jose Itzigsohn, "Immigration and Boundaries of Citizenship: The Institutions of Immigrants' Political Transnationalism," *International Migration Review* 34, no. 4 (2000): 1126–54. For a perspective from Turkish migrants in Germany: Eva Ostergaard-Nielson, "The Politics of Migrants' Transnational Practices," *International Migration Review* 37, no. 3 (2003): 760–86.

2. For evidence of this in Mexico see Robert C. Smith, "Migrant Membership as an Instituted Process: Transnationalization, the State, and the

Extra-Territorial Conduct of Mexican Politics," *International Migration Review* 37, no. 2 (2003): 297–343.

3. In fact, Levitt and Dehesa see this taking places in several Latin American countries. See Peggy Levitt and Rafael dela Dehesa, "Transnational Migration and the Redefinition of the State: Variations and Explanations," *Ethnic and Racial Studies* 26, no. 4 (2003): 587–611.

4. Saskia Sassen, *Territory, Authority, Rights: From Medieval to Global Assemblages* (Princeton: Princeton University Press, 2006): 17.

5. Aziz Choudry has examined the liberalization of the trade in services and its impacts on international labor migration. See his work in bilaterals.org/.

6. I discuss the Philippine state's role in the GFMD in more depth in "On the Question of Expertise: A Critical Reflection on 'Civil Society,' Processes," in *Learning from the Ground Up: Global Perspectives on Social Movements and Knowledge Production*, ed. Aziz Choudry and Dip Kapoor (New York: Palgrave Macmillan, forthcoming).

7. Yasmin Soysal, *The Limits of Citizenship: Migrants and Postnational Membership in Europe* (Chicago: University of Chicago Press, 1994).

8. This is what Kristen Hill Maher suggests in "Globalized Social Reproduction: Women Migrants and the Citizenship Gap," *People Out of Place: Globalization, Human Rights, and the Citizenship Gap*, ed. Alison Brysk and Gershon Shabir (New York: Routledge, 2004).

9. See my work on Migrante International: "Migrant Heroes: Nationalism, Citizenship, and the Politics of Filipino Migrant Labor," *Citizenship Studies* 6, no. 3 (2002): 341–56, and "Challenging the Limits of the Law," in *Globalization and Third World Women: Exploitation, Coping, and Resistance*, ed. Ligaya McGovern and Isidor Wallimann (Hampshire, U.K.: Ashgate Press, 2009): 49–63.

Index

abuse, 64, 104, 115, 121, 150–51; sexual, 93

adaptability, 50

advertisements: Able Minds, Able Hands to Foreign Lands (brochure), xi; colonial histories invoked in, 63; Filipino Nurses Caring for the World (brochure), 62; Filipino Workers Moving the World Today (brochure), 50, 51; Managing Labor Migration (brochure), 77

advertising strategies, 65

Aguilar, Filomeno, 85

Africa: as a destination for migrants, 20; POEA Marketing Branch regional desk for, 24

ambassadors of goodwill, 78

American colonialism, ix, xxv, 9; "benevolent assimilation" under, ix, 5; and Philippine educational system, ix

anti-Asian violence in the U.S., 4

Aquino, Corazon, 14–15, 152

Asia: International Labor Affairs offices in, 25; immigration restrictions in, 31, 43; labor attaché in, 24; labor market prospects of migrants to, 58; migrants bound for employment in, 163; newly industrialized countries in, 56; migration to, 20; Philippines as failed state of, xix; small and medium enterprises in, 56

Asia Pacific Economic Cooperation (APEC), 88, 146, 153

Asian Americans, 52

Asian crisis, 72

Asian migration to the U.S., 3

Asian workers' activism in the U.S., 4

Association of South East Asian States (ASEAN), 66–69, 146–48

authorization: migration bureaucracy and processes of, 21–22, 41–48, 53; and relations of trust between states, 22; state power of, 21–22, 142

Bagong Alyansang Makabayan (BAYAN), 152, 153

bagong bayani (new heroes), 84–85

balikbayan (nation returnee), 80–81, 159

Ball, Rochelle, 30

Bangladesh, 76, 123–26

bilateralism, 67, 122

bilateral labor agreements (BLA) 65–69, 72–74, 109, 118, 120, 122, 140

Bourdieu, Pierre, 21

brochures, xi, 50–53, 61, 65. See also advertisements

Brooks, Ethel, 62, 63

Brown, Wendy, 104

Brunei, 55, 149; activism of migrants in, 124–25, 131–39, 149; employment in, 54, 116–19, 139; Labor Department, 127–28; labor recruitment agencies to, 132; Philippine diplomatic relations with, 120, 127–9, 131, 140

Bureau of Employment Services (BES), 12

Robyn Magalit Rodriguez is assistant professor of sociology at Rutgers University.